Contemporary Architect's Concept Series 1

Sou Fujimoto: Primitive Future

INAX Publishing

Contemporary Architect's Concept Series 1
Sou Fujimoto: Primitive Future

First published in Japan on April 15, 2008 by INAX Publishing.

INAX Publishing: 3-6-18 Kyobashi, Chuo-ku, Tokyo 104-0031, Japan
TEL: +81 03 5250 6571   FAX: +81 03 5250 6549
http://www.inax.co.jp/Culture/top/pub.html

Authors: Sou Fujimoto, Toyo Ito, Taro Igarashi, Terunobu Fujimori
Publisher: Izumi Akiyama
Editing and Planning by Media Design Research Ltd.
Book Designed by Satoshi Machiguchi / match and company, inc.
Printed by Toppan Printing Co., Ltd.

© 2008 by Sou Fujimoto

All rights reserved. No part of this book may be reproduced or utilized in any form or by any information storage and retrieval system, without prior permission in writing from the copyright holders.

2008 Printed in Japan ISBN978-4-87275-148-2 C0352

藤本壮介　│　原初的な未来の建築

INAX出版

CONTENTS

藤本壮介とは何者か？— I

6 ── 「弱い建築」からの脱皮

伊東豊雄 ［いとう・とよお／建築家］

Who is Sou Fujimoto? — I

9 ── Casting off "Weak Architecture"

Toyo Ito ［Architect］

Translated by Thomas Daniell

藤本壮介とは何者か？— II

12 ── 直角のない幾何学

五十嵐太郎 ［いがらし・たろう／建築史・建築批評］

Who is Sou Fujimoto? — II

15 ── Geometry without Right Angles

Taro Igarashi ［Architectural historian, Critic］

Translated by Thomas Daniell

18 ── 藤本壮介　原初的な未来の建築

Sou Fujimoto: Primitive Future

Translated by Kaz Yoneda

124 ── 人工の建築、自然の建築

対談：藤森照信 ［ふじもり・てるのぶ／建築史・建築家］× 藤本壮介

136 ── Artificial Architecture,
Natural Architecture: Dialogue Summary

Terunobu Fujimori ［Architectural historian, Architect］× Sou Fujimoto

Translated by Kaz Yoneda

140 ── Data

142 ── Profile / Photo Credit

藤本壮介とは何者か？──Ⅰ

「弱い建築」からの脱皮

伊東豊雄［いとう・とよお／建築家］

藤本壮介といえば、「青森県立美術館」コンペティション（2000）［pp.60, 62］のことを想い出す。2次審査まで残り、インタヴューに現われた時、彼は未だ29歳で、私は審査員長を務めていた。黒川紀章や青木淳、千葉学等の提案者に伍して、彼はたったひとりで飄々と登場し、いきなり「僕は弱い建築をつくりたいのです」と語り始めた。気負うことなく終始笑顔で淡々とコンセプトを語る姿に、審査員たちは呆気にとられた。
最終的には僅差で青木淳に最優秀賞の座を奪われたのだが、彼の明晰な語り口は後々まで強く印象に残った。
この時藤本が語った「弱い建築」とは、彼の解説によれば、「大きな秩序からではなく、部分と部分の関係性から建築をつくっていくこと」であり、それによって「不確定性とか乱雑さとか、そういうものを内包している秩序をつくり得る」（TNプローブ連続レクチャー「オルタナティブ・モダン」より）のである。
確かに「青森県立美術館」の藤本案は片流れの屋根を持つ小さなヴォリュームが接しながらさまざまな角度で連続し、全体はゆるい関係で統合されている。軸線はもちろんのこと、グリッドのように全体を一挙に決定づけてしまう規則性とは対極の構成である。ただ隣接するヴォリューム相互の「謙虚にして、かつ適切なる関係」のみによって全体がレイアウトされている。
だが全体を一挙に統合してしまう軸やグリッドを回避するのは理解できるとしても、「謙虚にして適切なる関係」とは何か。そこに何らかの「ゆるい秩序」は存在するのだろうか。彼はいまのところこの秩序を、それ以上に説き明かそうとはしない。単に自然界のものの存在の関係に喩えるだけである。自然界のものの関係はすべて相対的であり、それらはゆる

く、しかし微妙かつ繊細に関係づけられている。彼は自らの繊細な感受性を以て、そうした自然界のものの関係を感じ取り、それを建築の図式として描こうとしているように思われる。

このような繊細な感受性が最大限に発揮されたのが《T House》(2005)［pp.45, 47］である。群馬県の地方都市に実現したこの住宅は延床面積わずか90㎡の平屋である。微妙な角度で折れ曲がる外側は青黒い板貼りの壁に囲まれて飾り気のない佇まいを見せている。外に向けられた開口は小さく少ない。

しかし一歩内部に足を入れた途端に、訪れた人はいままで経験したことのない空間の多様さに驚かされる。ここには狭小さと広がり、単純さと複雑さ、貧しさと豊かさ等、相反する要素が同時存在している。

空間の多様さを生み出しているのは、まず第一に独特な平面の分割にある。親子4人のための居住空間は放射状に分割されているのだが、ほとんどすべての部屋はオープンで、全体はワンルームとも言える。すなわち各部屋は三方は壁に囲まれているのだが、残り一面は中央に向かって開かれている。しかし放射状とは言っても、壁のラインはきわめて繊細に方向を調整されており、室相互は実に微妙に見え隠れする。一歩移動するだけで各室間の関係は変化するのである。

藤本はこの関係を「距離感の建築」と語っている。彼にとっては「物理的な距離ではなく、むしろ空間のゆがみや抑揚によって生まれる体験的、相対的な距離」(『新建築』2005年5月)こそが意味を持つのである。

そしてその距離の関係を一層際立たせているのが壁の薄さである。放射状に引かれたラインを立ち上げている壁はわずか12㎜厚の構造用合板である。片側にリブが添えられなければ座屈してしまいそうな薄さである。だがこの薄い壁を用いることによって、空間の緊張感は一気に高まった。住人も訪れた人も、この内部では動物的な本能を蘇らされる。さまざまな関係に対して気配で反応するしかないからである。

藤本壮介はきわめて論理的に語ることのできる建築家であるが、他方で類いまれな感受性を備えた建築家である。あれほどに質素な素材を用いてこれほど豊かな空間を生む才能は動物的ともいえる感覚にある。

藤本は自らの建築におけるものの関係をしばしば5線譜のない音符に喩える。空気のような見えないモジュールに基づくものの配列を生み出しているのは、彼の内部に存在する動物的なカンでしかないだろう。それをあえて説明する必要はないが、これまで私が気にかかっていたのは、彼が要素として何気なく用いるキューブのことである。例えば《情緒障害児短期治療施設》(2006)［pp.28-31, 50-55］は群をなすホワイトキューブの配列がテーマである。微妙な角度と距離をもって配置されたキューブは美しい集落のような佇まいを示している。キューブは関係を生み出す要素以上の意味を持たないのかもしれない。だがキューブは所詮キューブである。モダニズムの建築が背負ってきたキューブの意味から逃れるわけにはいかないだろう。ミニマリズムやピュアな幾何学といったモダニズムの文脈で受け取られても仕方がないのである。

こんな疑問を抱いていた時に、「熊本アートポリス次世代木造バンガロー」プロジェクト（2005-08）［p.121］が登場した。これもまたキューブである。しかも1個だけのキューブである。だがこのキューブはホワイトキューブではない。35cm角の木材のみを積層させ、内部をえぐって洞窟のような空間をつくり出しているマッシヴなキューブである。太い角材は構造材を形成するのは言うまでもないが、時には腰を下ろすベンチや食卓となり、ベッドにもなる。実に骨太で力強いキューブが実現しつつあるのだ。

最早や「弱い建築」どころではない。プリミティヴな木材の香りで充満する嗅覚的建築であり、木の質感が身体の奥深くまで浸透する触覚的建築である。おそらくこのプロジェクトが実現することによって、藤本壮介の動物的な感受性はより逞しく生長するに違いない。今後のプロジェクトにその逞しさがいかに表現されるのか、今から待たれるところである。

Who is Sou Fujimoto? — I

Casting off "Weak Architecture"

Toyo Ito [Architect]

Translated by Thomas Daniell

When I hear Sou Fujimoto's name, I remember the Aomori Prefectural Art Museum Design Competition (2000) [pp.60, 62]. Having lasted until the second round of judging, at the time of the interview he was still only 29 years old and I was serving as the head of the jury. He held his own against proposals from figures such as Kisho Kurokawa, Jun Aoki, and Manabu Chiba. Appearing alone and aloof, he began by suddenly saying, "I want to make weak architecture." Without becoming agitated, smiling from beginning to end, he nonchalantly talked about his concept, leaving the judges dumbfounded by his manner.

Jun Aoki finally took the first prize by a narrow margin, but his clear way of talking left a powerful and lasting impression.

According to Fujimoto's own explanation, the notion of "weak architecture" that he was then talking about is "not making architecture from an overall order but from the relationships between each of the parts," and as a result, "an order can be made that incorporates uncertainty or disorder" (From the TN Probe lecture series *Alternative Modern*).

To be sure, the small volumes with monopitch roofs in Fujimori's proposal for the Aomori Prefectural Art Museum are connected at various angles and the whole is integrated by loose relationships. This is the antithesis of a compositional rule that instantaneously determines the whole, like a grid or an axis. The whole is laid out with no more than "modest and appropriate relationships" between the adjacent volumes.

But even if the avoidance of an axis or grid that instantaneously integrates the whole is comprehensible, what are these "modest and appropriate relationships"? Does some kind of "loose order" exist there? At present, he doesn't try to explain anything more than this order. He simply compares it to the relationships that exist between things in the natural world. The relationships of things in the natural world are all contingent. They are loose, but subtly and delicately interrelated. By means of his own delicate sensitivity he seems to feel the relationships of things in the natural world, and attempts to delineate them as architectural diagrams.

It is in the T House (2005) [pp.45, 47] that this delicate sensitivity is given maximum expression. Realized in a provincial city in Gunma Prefecture, this is a one-story house with a total floor area of only 90m^2. Enclosed by walls clad in blue-black panels, the subtly angled exterior presents a sober appearance. The apertures facing the outside are small and few.

Yet in the act of setting foot inside, visitors are astonished by the unprecedented spatial variety. Compression and expansion, simplicity and complexity, poverty and richness: reciprocal elements exist here simultaneously.

The first step in creating spatial variety is the distinctive subdivision of the plan. Though this residential space for a family of four is partitioned radially, almost all the rooms are open, and the whole could also be called a single space. That is to say, each room is enclosed by walls on three sides but the remaining side is open toward the center. Yet even though I described it as radial, the directions of the wall lines have been adjusted with extreme delicacy, and in fact the rooms subtly and appear and disappear. The relationships between all the rooms are altered by taking a single step.

Fujimoto talks about this relationship as "architecture with a sense of distance." For him, this means "not a physical distance, but an experiential, relational distance that arises due to the distortion and modulation of the space" (*Shinkenchiku*, May 2005).

This relationship of distance is made even more conspicuous by the thinness of the walls. The walls standing upon these radially drawn lines are merely 12mm-thick plywood, and are used as the structure. The thinness suggests they would buckle if not supported by ribs on one face. However, the sense of tension in the space is instantly increased by the use of these thin walls. In this interior, the animalistic instincts of the inhabitants as well as the visitors are revived. That's because they can do nothing but react to hints about the various interrelationships. Sou Fujimoto is an architect able to talk extremely logically, but on other hand he is an architect endowed with a rare sensitivity. That's why he has the talent to create such rich spaces using such frugal materials, with what might be called an animalistic feeling.

Fujimoto frequently compares the relationships between things in his own architecture to musical notes without a score. Arranging things based on a module that is as invisible as air probably originates from an animalistic intuition within Fujimoto's subconscious. There's no need to dare trying to explain this, but I have been uneasy about his casual use of cubes as elements. For example, the theme of his Children's Center for Psychiatric Rehabilitation (2006) [pp.28-31, 50-55] is an array of white cubes. The cubes are arranged with subtle angles and distances, presenting the appearance of a beautiful village. The cubes might possess no meaning beyond being elements that produce relationships. Yet a cube is, after all, a cube. It's impossible to escape the meaning of the cubes on which modernist architecture was predicated. Even taken in the modernist context of minimalism and pure geometry, this is unavoidable.

While I was harboring these doubts, I was confronted with the Next Generation Wooden Bungalows project (2005-08) [p.121]. This is also a cube. Moreover, it is only one cube. Yet this cube isn't a white cube. It's a massive cube comprising nothing more than layered 35cm-square pieces of timber, from which a cave-like space has been produced by scooping out the interior. Needless to say, the thick rectangular pieces of timber form the structure, but at times they also become a bench, a dining table, and a bed. A truly stout, powerful cube is being manifested. This is absolutely not the "weak architecture" he has been doing up until now. A fragrant architecture suffused with the primitive smell of timber, this is also a tactile architecture wherein the qualities of the wood deeply penetrate the human body. The realization of this project will surely cause Sou Fujimoto's animalistic sensitivity to grow more robust. I am now waiting to see how this robustness will be expressed in his future projects.

藤本壮介とは何者か？——Ⅱ

直角のない幾何学

五十嵐太郎［いがらし・たろう／建築史・建築批評］

最後の建築家

藤本壮介は、「最後の建築家」として登場した。
『建築文化』2003年8月号（彰国社）の「特集＝U-35のポテンシャル」にあわせて開催されたシンポジウムにおいて、この言葉は使われた。コンピュータを駆使して情報環境をフィールドとする3名の若手、2名の構造家、そして組織設計事務所のパネリストが続き、最後に彼の順番がまわったせいもある。もはや次世代の建築は、旧来のデザインとは全然違う世界に突入するのか。会場がそんな雰囲気になったとき、彼は「最後の建築家」として語りはじめた。建築の教育を受けたものが建築の外部に関心を抱く時代にあえて、建築にこだわること。新しい世紀を迎え、何もかもが未知のものへと向かって、まっしぐらになっていたとき、藤本は、はるか彼方の昔から続くもっとも古いテクノロジーのひとつである建築の根源に向きあう。だが、それは単純な過去への回帰でもない。
有名な「藤本マンダラ」の図を見ると、設計者の名もわからぬコロッセウムや法隆寺、あるいはミース・ファン・デル・ローエの《新国立美術館》のプランと一緒に自作をまぎれこませ、彼が時空を超えた歴史意識をもっていることがうかがえる。もっとも、ポストモダン的な過去の記号の引用ではない。抽象化された形式のレヴェルにおいて過去と現代を並列している。実際、藤本の建築は、過度に最新のテクノロジーに頼るデザインを行なわないために、過去にも存在しえたものになっている。「安中環境アートフォーラム」のコンペ案（2003）［p.44, 46］のように、壁の構成を主軸とする作品は、組積造のイメージすらただよう。むろん、屋根をかける場合は、現代のテクノロジーが必要になるだろうが、壁の建築としては、2,000年前でも可能だったのではないかと思わせる空間の形式であ

る。《T House》(2005) [p.45, 47] も、薄い木の壁によって構成された平屋だが、アイディアさえあれば、木造の文化圏において近代以前にも構想しえたデザインではないかと、ふと想像したくなる。

1990年代の後半、アトリエ・ワンやみかんぐみなど、複数の建築家がチームを組むユニット派と呼ばれる世代が頭角を現わした。1960年代生まれの彼らは都市を観察し、さまざまな状況や外在的な条件から日常性の感覚をもつ建築を導きだす。バブル経済の時代に流行した自意識過剰なポストモダンに反発したことが、こうした態度を招いたのである。ユニット派は、英雄的な建築家のふるまいや、フィクション性が強い形態操作を好まない。しかし、藤本は、ルイス・カーンやル・コルビュジエなどの巨匠を直接的に意識している。彼を含めて、石上純也、平田晃久などの1970年代生まれの建築家は、個人の活動が目立つ。彼らは、まわりの敷地を説明してから建築を組立てることよりも、ストレートに新しい建築の原理そのものをつかみだそうとしている。そして光の見え方や複数の人の関係性など、固有の場において生起する現象の経験に大きな興味をもつ。藤本は、ユニット派以降の次世代の動向を牽引するもっとも重要な建築家である。

コロンブスの卵

初めて《Tokyo Apartment》(2006-09) [p.111, 114-115] の模型を見たときの衝撃を忘れられない。いくつもの家型のヴォリュームを無造作に積みあげた信じがたい風景。ポストモダンの建築家のように、脱構築主義の哲学やアヴァンギャルドの芸術を参照する必要はない。おそろしく簡単な操作によって、家型という見慣れた形象がまったく違う姿となって立ち上がる。だが、いったん新しい発見が提示されると、なんだこんなことかと、あたりまえのようにわれわれはそれを共有できてしまう。藤本がもたらす驚きは、コロンブスの卵を思わせる。同じエピソードはルネサンスの建築家ブルネレスキのヴァージョンでも知られているが、ともあれ、誰にでもできそうなことを最初にやってしまう天才的なひらめきをもつ。ところで、以前、筆者はどうやって人類は最初に直角を発見したのかを

めぐって、あるアーティストと議論したことがあった。もちろん、正解はないだろう。そのときさまざまな誕生の場面を想定したのだが、部分からモノをつくる段階では、それほど直角が必要ないという仮説を立てた。しかし、全体をつくる、あるいは想定してから、単位を分割したり、単位をきれいに組み合わせて、全体を整えるというときに、どうしても直角が登場するのではないか。なるほど、洞窟やプリミティヴな集落など、最初期の空間においてあまり直角は使われない。厳密な直角をもたない空間は、「建築」以前というべきか。

おそらく、こうした直角の問題は、藤本がよく言う「部分の建築」の考えにもつながる。「安中環境アートフォーラム」では、不定形の空間を押したり、ひっぱることで生成する、ぐにゃぐにゃの輪郭をもつ空間を提案した。内側から膨らんでいきながら生成したかのような《T House》のプランも、壁を崩れた放射状に配置し、直角を拒否している。《伊達の援護寮》(2003)[p. 56-57]、《情緒障害児短期治療施設》(2006)[pp. 28-31, 50-55]、「青森県立美術館」のコンペ案(2000)[pp. 60, 62]などは、個の単位に直角を使うものの、非直角による連結のシステムを採用した。こうした手法が、彼の建築に対し、見たことがないのに、太古のようなものを思わせる要因になっている。

藤本の狙いは、幾何学が成立する座標系＝フィールドそのものを刷新することである。それゆえ、筆者が企画したKPOキリンプラザ大阪の「ニュージオメトリーの建築――もうひとつのモダニズムをめざして」展(2006)では、彼に参加を依頼した。藤本が1/1の模型として制作した《House OM》は、大きな壁が一筆書きですべて連続しており、二重のリングが絡みあうようなプランをもつ。やはり直角がない。壁が交わるところは、それぞれの上下に大きな開口をとって、閉鎖的になることを避けている。その結果、内部と外部が相互貫入するチューブ状の空間が展開した。部屋の区切りはなく、全体がうねる廊下のようにつながる。直角や平行線によって建築に明快な秩序を与えるのが普通の幾何学だとすれば、新しい幾何学はシンプルでありながら、複雑で多様な場を生む。藤本は、直角以前の感性を導入することで、現代的な空間の感覚をもたらす。

Who is Sou Fujimoto? — II

Geometry without Right Angles

Taro Igarashi [Architectural historian, Critic]

Translated by Thomas Daniell

The Last Architect

Sou Fujimoto made his appearance as "the last architect."
That phrase was used at a symposium on the theme of "the potential of the under-35s," held in conjunction with the August 2003 issue of the magazine *Kenchiku Bunka* (Shokokusha). Following a series of three young computer experts working in the field of information environments, two structural engineers, and a panelist from a corporate architecture office, it was finally his turn. Had the architecture of the next generation already plunged into a world completely detached from traditional design? That was the atmosphere of the venue when he began to speak as "the last architect." In an era where people with an architectural education are focusing on areas outside the field of architecture, he has defiantly clung to architecture. While charging into the new century, with almost everything we confront still unknown, Fujimoto has turned to the roots of architecture as one of the oldest technologies from the far distant past. But this is not a simple revival of the past.

Looking at the famous "Fujimoto mandala" drawing, in which he intermingles his own work with the Coliseum and Horyuji Temple, their designers unknown, or the plan of Mies van der Rohe's Neue Nationalgalerie, it is clear he possesses an awareness of history that exceeds space and time. Yet this is not a postmodernist quotation of symbols from the past. At the level of abstracted form, he puts the past and the present in parallel. In fact, because his designs do not rely on cutting-edge technology, Fujimoto's architecture could have also existed in the past. It is suffused with the imagery of masonry construction, as with the Annaka Art Forum competition proposal (2003) [pp.44, 46], a work that takes the layout of the walls as its principle element. Obviously, modern technology might be needed if a roof is placed on top, but as an architecture of walls, I wonder if its spatial schema might have been possible even 2,000 years ago. The T House (2005) [pp.45, 47] is a one-story house composed of thin wood walls, but I can immediately imagine that the design concept could also have been achieved within the premodern cultural sphere of wooden construction, if someone only had the idea.

In the latter half of the 1990s, a generation appeared that was characterised by multiple architects joining together in teams such as Atelier Bow-Wow and Mikan, which became known as yunitto-ha. Born in the 1960s, they observed the city, and derived architecture possessing a sensibility of daily life from various conditions and external requirements. Their attitude was a consequence of revulsion for the ego-driven postmodernism that had been fashionable during the economic bubble period. The yunitto-ha abhor the heroic behavior of architects and their fantastical manipulations of form. Fujimoto, however, has a direct awareness of the great masters such as Louis Kahn and Le Corbusier. Like him, architects born in the 1970s such as Junya Ishigami and Akihisa Hirata are conspicuously working alone. Rather than assembling architecture after having explained the surrounding site, they seem to have a direct grasp of the principles for making new architecture. They have a strong interest in the experience of phenomena that occur in specific places, such as the way light is seen or the relationships between people. In defining the attitudes of the generation that has followed the yunitto-ha, Fujimoto is an extremely important architect,

The Egg of Columbus

I will never forget the shock I felt the first time I saw the model of the Tokyo Apartment (2006-09) [pp.111, 114-115]. It is an implausible scene of many house-shaped volumes nonchalantly stacked up. There's no need to study the philosophy of deconstruction or to refer to avant-garde art, as with postmodern architects. By the same simple operation, the familiar image of a house shape is assembled into a completely different profile. But at the very moment a new discovery is presented – what's that! – we become able to share it as something completely obvious. The surprises provoked by Fujimoto recall the tale of the Egg of Columbus. A version of that same anecdote is told about the Renaissance architect Brunelleschi, but in any case, for something that looks like anyone could have done it, the first person to actually do it has shown a spark of genius.

Incidentally, I previously debated how the human race might have discovered the right angle, in an argument with a particular artist. Of course, there is probably no correct answer. At that time, we envisioned a variety of genesis scenes, but we speculated that a right angle wouldn't be necessary at the stage of making a thing from parts. However, after the whole has been made or hypothesized, it might be divided into units, then those units cleanly assembled, so it seems probable that right angles would unavoidably appear when preparing the whole. Admittedly, right angles were rarely used in the earliest spaces of caves and primitive villages. Should a space without strict right angles be described as prior to "architecture"?

Perhaps this problem of the right angle is connected to the idea of an "architecture of parts" that Fujimoto often mentions. The Annaka Environmental Art Forum is a proposal for a space with an amorphous profile, in which protean spaces are generated by processes of pushing and pulling. The plan of the T House also seems to have been generated while it was swelling from the inside, the walls collapsing into a radial arrangement that rejects right angles. The Rehabilitation Dormitory in Hokkaido (2003) [p.56-57], the Children's Center for Psychiatric Rehabilitation (2006) [pp.28-31, 50-55], and the Aomori Prefectural Art Museum Competition (2000) [pp.60, 62] each adopt a system of non-right angle connections for individual units that use right angles. For his architecture, this method seems unprecedented yet its parameters recall the ancient past.

Fujimoto's aim is to transform the geometry that underlies the coordinate system, which is equivalent to the field itself. That is why I invited him to participate in an exhibition I organized at Kirin Plaza Osaka, entitled *New Geometry Architecture: Toward an Alternative Modernism* (2006). Fujimoto produced a full-size model of the House OM, in which a large, entirely continuous wall is intertwined to create a double-ring plan. As I expected, there were no right angles. By making large openings at the places where the wall intersects, it avoided becoming overly closed. As a result, it expanded into a tubular space with mutual interpenetration of inside and outside. With no delimitation of rooms, the whole was connected like an undulating passage. If ordinary geometry gives a lucid order to architecture by means of right angles and parallel lines, new geometry may be simple but gives birth to complex and diverse places. By introducing a sensitivity that predates the right angle, Fujimoto provides a contemporary spatial sensibility.

1 Nest or Cave

2 Notes without Staves - The New Geometry

3 Separation and Connection

4 City as House - House as City

5 In a Tree-like Place

6 Nebulous

7 Gürü - Gürü

8 Garden

9 Before House and City and Forest

10 Before Matter and Space

Sou Fujimoto
Primitive Future

新しい建築、未来の建築を考えるということは、奇妙なことに、原初的な建築を考えるということと表裏ではないだろうか。なぜなら建築は、人がいる場所だから。そして建築の新しさの提案は、人のいる場所として根源的な新しさであってほしいから。

建築が建築になる以前にさかのぼる。そして建築の始まる瞬間に立ち返る。さかのぼるといっても、ローマ、ギリシアという歴史をさかのぼるのではない。人のいる場所のかすかな始まりに思いを馳せ、あいまいな、ぼんやりした場の起伏のなかから、建築がにじみ出てくる瞬間を想像する。

ここでは、10の建築の始まりが描かれている。

建築の、というよりも、人のいる場所としての、圧倒的に未分化な状態にさかのぼる。それぞれの始まりからは無数の違った建築が生まれてくる。違っているけれども、それぞれは互いに関係しあっている。この始まりは予感である。ひとつの正しい始まりではなくて無数の始まりを許容する予感。

だから未来の建築を考えるということは原初的である。人がいる場所とはどんなものなのか、建築とはこんなものでもあったのかと想像する。原初的な未来は、そんな喜びにあふれている。

To consider innovative architecture of the future is astonishingly equivalent to reflect on primitive architecture. That is because architecture transpires wherever people exist. Thus, novel architecture must be a conception of a place for humanity that is fundamentally new.

Imagine going back in time before architecture became architecture, and standing at the exact moment when architecture began. This is not to retrace the ancient history of Rome or Greece; rather, it is to envision the moment architecture emerged from the fluctuations of a nebulous, protean field together with a vague and originary trace of human domain.

Here are the ten geneses of architecture. Transcending architecture, they trace back the conditions of human habitation to an overwhelmingly embryonic state.

Each starting-point gives birth to myriads of different architecture. Each outcome is unique, yet related amongst each another. These beginnings are intuitions; a hunch that there are infinite points of departure instead of one righteous beginning.

Thus, to speculate on the future of architecture is equally primordial. Imagine the diversity of places people can inhabit, and the possibilities of what architecture may become. Primitive future is full of promising projections.

1 巣ではなく洞窟のような
Nest or Cave

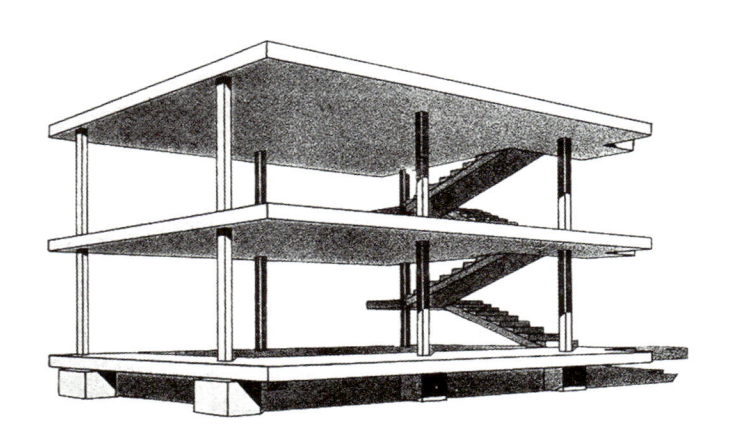

NEST

CAVE

「巣」と「洞窟」という2つの始まりを考えてみる。
巣とは、住み手が自分に快適なように場所をしつらえ、作り上げるものである。
機能主義の原型。一方で洞窟は、もともとそこにある。
住み手にとって良いとか悪いとか、そういうこととは関係なしに、ただそこにある。
その中に人は入って行き、さまざまな凹凸やスケールなどの手がかりを
自分で解釈しながら住みこなしていく。他者としての建築。
「住むための機械」と言ったル・コルビュジエは
人間のための巣を提示した。僕は、そこからさらにさかのぼって、
巣になる直前の「洞窟」としての建築を模索する。
機能という名において整理するのではなく、人にさまざまに働きかける
きっかけに満ちた場所。機能を強制するのではなく、誘発し、許容する場。
単なる自然でもなく、単なる人工物でもなく、人工と自然のあいだとでもいうべき、
新しい建築のあり方を模索する。

Consider the two origins of a "Nest" and a "Cave."
As a functionalist archetype, a nest is prepared according to inhabitants'
sense of comfortability while a cave exists regardless of convenience or otherwise to its inhabitants;
it remains indifferent. Upon entering a cave, humanity adeptly assimilated to the landscape by
interpreting the various hints of convexo-concave surfaces and scales.
This is architecture of unrelated external factors.
Le Corbusier, who proclaimed "Machine for Living," devised a nest for people.
Tracing further back, I envision architecture as a cave immediately before becoming a nest.
It is not organized in the name of functionalism but by place-making that
encourages people to seek a spectrum of opportunities.
Instead of oppressing functions, a cave is a provocative and unrestricted milieu.
Neither purely natural nor purely artificial, I search for an ideal
condition of new architecture in between artifice and nature.

Primitive Future House, project, 2001

35cmの段差によってできた地形。
家具であり建築でありランドスケープであるような場所。
透明で人工的な洞窟の提案。

This topography is composed of 35 cm increments. Not dissimilar to landscape, it is simultaneously furniture as well as architecture. It is a proposition for a transparent and artificial cave.

2 5線のない楽譜／新しい幾何学
Notes without Staves - The New Geometry

Aria mit verschiedenen Veränderungen
BWV 988

Johann Sebastian Bach
1685-1750

Mies

Aria mit verschiedenen Veränderungen
BWV 988

Aria

Johann Sebastian Bach
1685-1750

?

5線とそれを仕切る小節線。

バロック期に確立したこの譜面には、絶対時間と均質空間が可視化されている。

まず、時間が流れている。その上に僕たちはさまざまな音や活動を配置していく。

近代の時間観・空間観。ミース・ファン・デル・ローエ。

5線のない楽譜を描いてみる。人為的な秩序から解放された、

名づけようのない複雑な秩序とともに音符が立ち現われる。

ここには背後に流れる時間は存在しない。音と、次の音との関係のなかに、

初めて個別の時間が流れはじめる。音と時間は同時に生まれ、空間とものたちは同時に響き始める。

そもそも音楽とは、そして空間とは、そういうものではなかったか。

時間は、つまり空間は、関係性である。建築の新しい秩序を予感する。

Five staves divided by measures.
The ubiquitous musical notation system, established during the
Baroque Period, signified the absolute time and a homogenous space.
In musical notation, time is unidirectionally flowing. On that,
we superimpose our sounds and activities.
This was the Modernist temporality and spatiality of Mies van der Rohe.
Draw the notes without staves. Notes emerged as though by an
ineffably complex system liberated from the anthropogenic order.
Here, the undercurrent of time ceases to exist. The interactions
between notes activate the heretofore unimaginable multidirectional
flows of independent times. As sound and time were synchronically born,
space and objects resonate in unison.
Were not music and space always as such?
Time, and thus space, is comprised of various relationships.
New order of architecture is emerging.

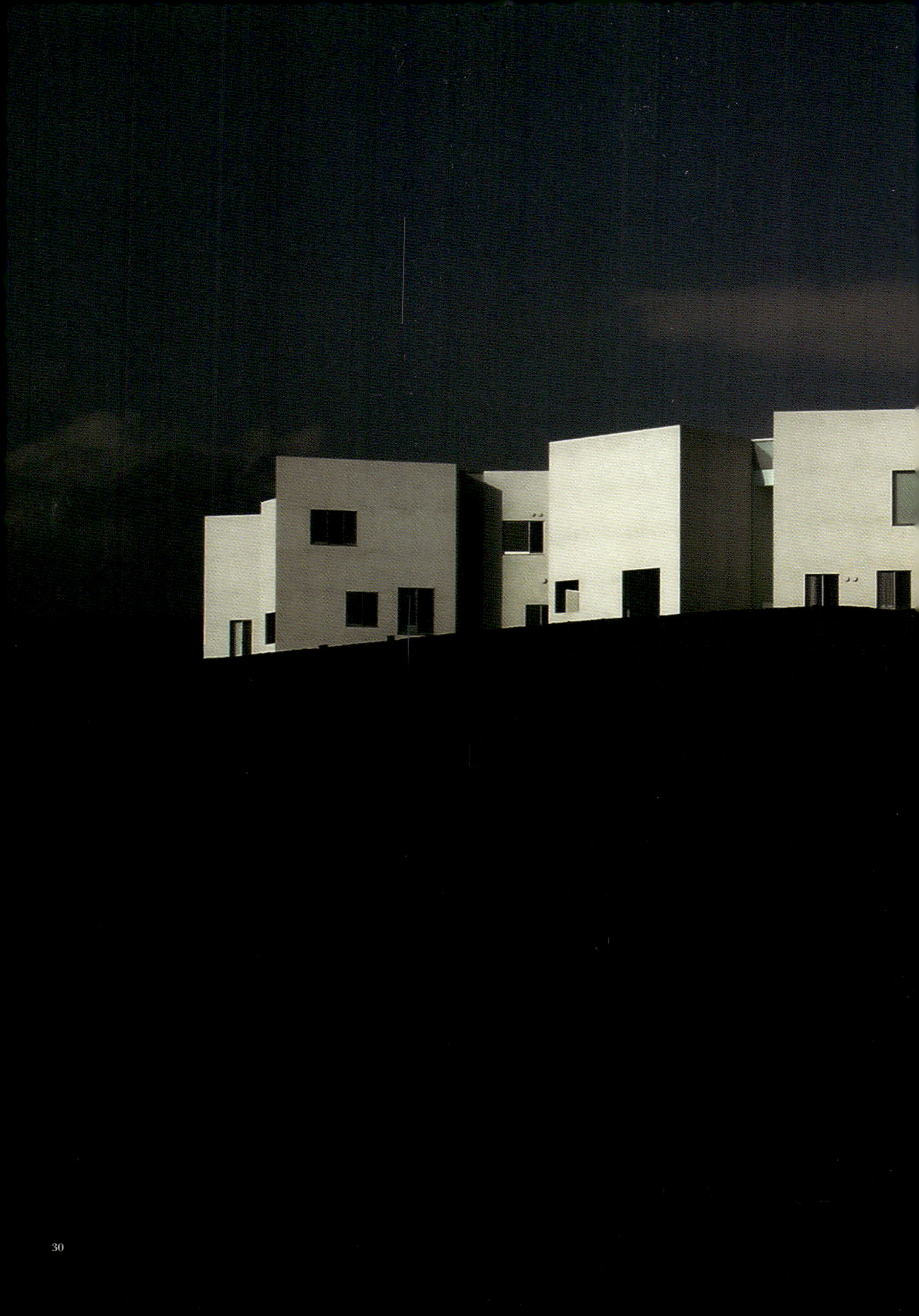

Children's Center for Psychiatric Rehabilitation, 2006

3 離れていて同時に繋がっている
Separation and Connection

「空間とは関係性である」。
そうだとするなら建築とは距離感を作り出すことであろう。
建築の始まりには、ただ「距離感」だけがあったに違いない。
壁や屋根が生まれるはるか以前に、さまざまな距離感の抑揚のみが
意識されていたに違いない。距離感とは人と人、ものともの、人とものの関係性であり、
可能性としての距離感が豊かな空間は、多様な質のグラデーション、
イントネーションに満ちているだろう。
離れているけれども繋がっている。
近いけれども離れている。気配で繋がっている。
そしてその関係性は移動を伴って刻々と変わっていく。
その距離感の起伏のなかに、人は住むための場所を見出していく。

"Space is Relationships."
Architecture is to generate various senses of distances.
The origin of architecture must have been constituted purely of "distances."
Far before the advent of roofs or walls, only the various modulations of distances were recognized.
Distance predicated the degrees of interactions amongst persons and
objects; thus, the profound spatial expressions of potential
expanses were enriched by diverse qualities of gradations and intonations.
One can be alienated and yet connected. Close and yet separate.
Associations are solely indicated by propinquity.
These interactions transformed ad infinitum with motion.
People can discover places for habitation in those cadences of space.

Seidai Hospital New Wing, project, 2006–

House O, 2007

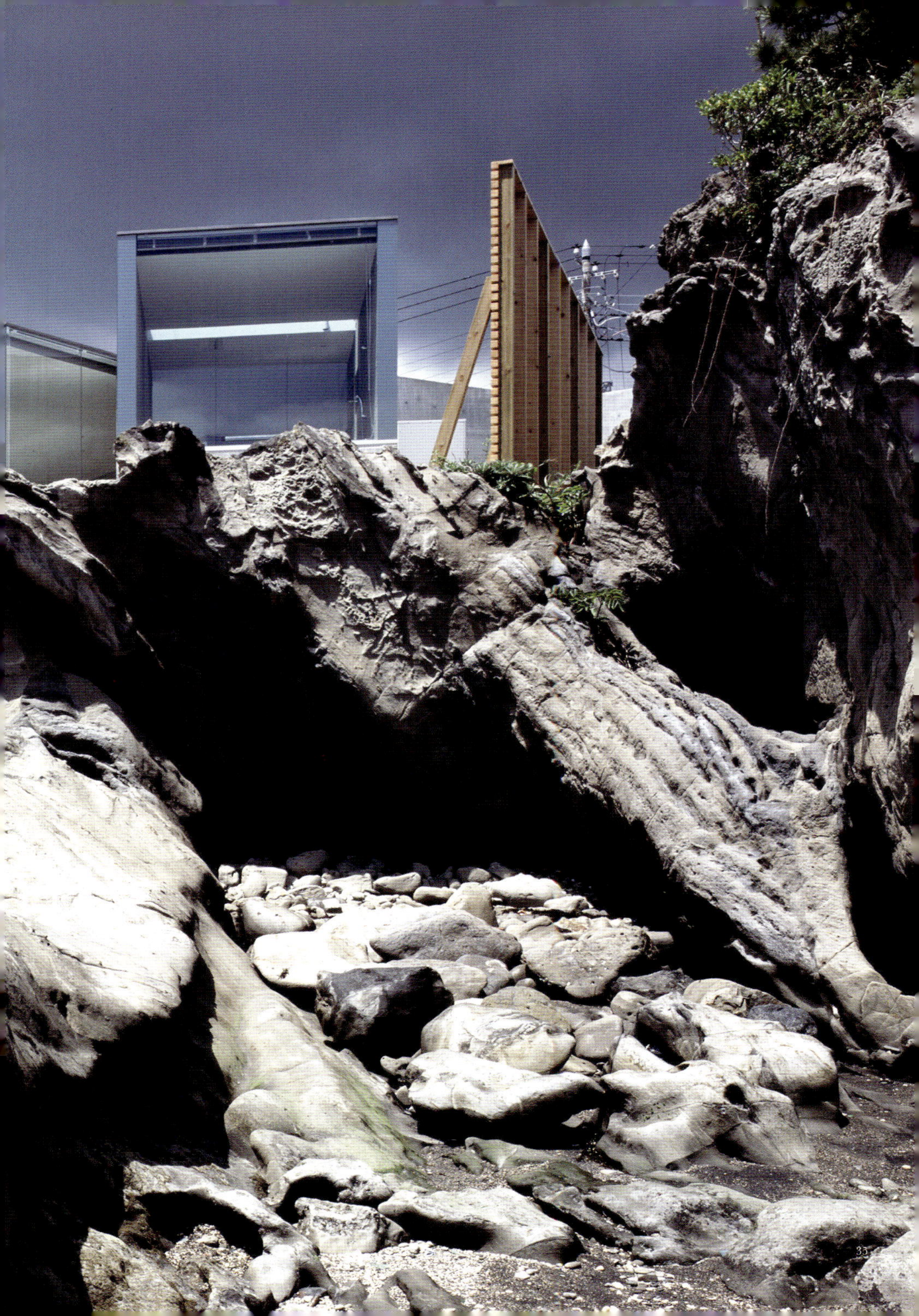

壁を立てることは、空間を０か１かに分けてしまう。

To erect a wall is to bisect a space into 0 and 1.

でも本当は、空間には、0と1の間のグラデーションの豊かさがあるはずだ。

However, a space must have intrinsically had rich gradations between 0 and 1.

House O

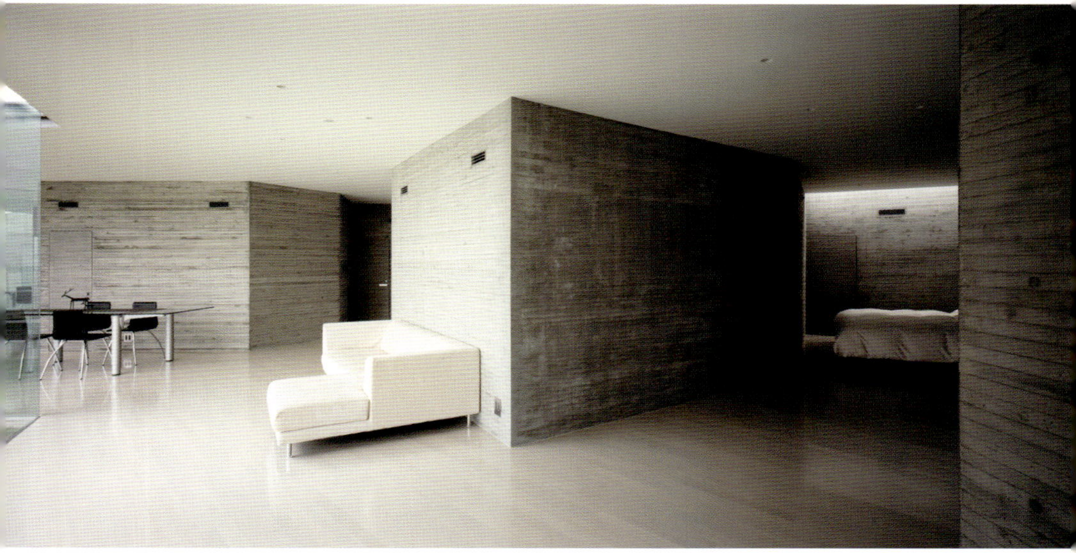

岩場に建つ住宅、ではなく、場の質として、岩場的なる住宅。
岩場には、隠れる場所、開けた場所、向かい合って座れる場所、寄りかかるくぼみ、
よじ登る小山……、いろいろな場所がある。
岩場は光に満ちた洞窟である。

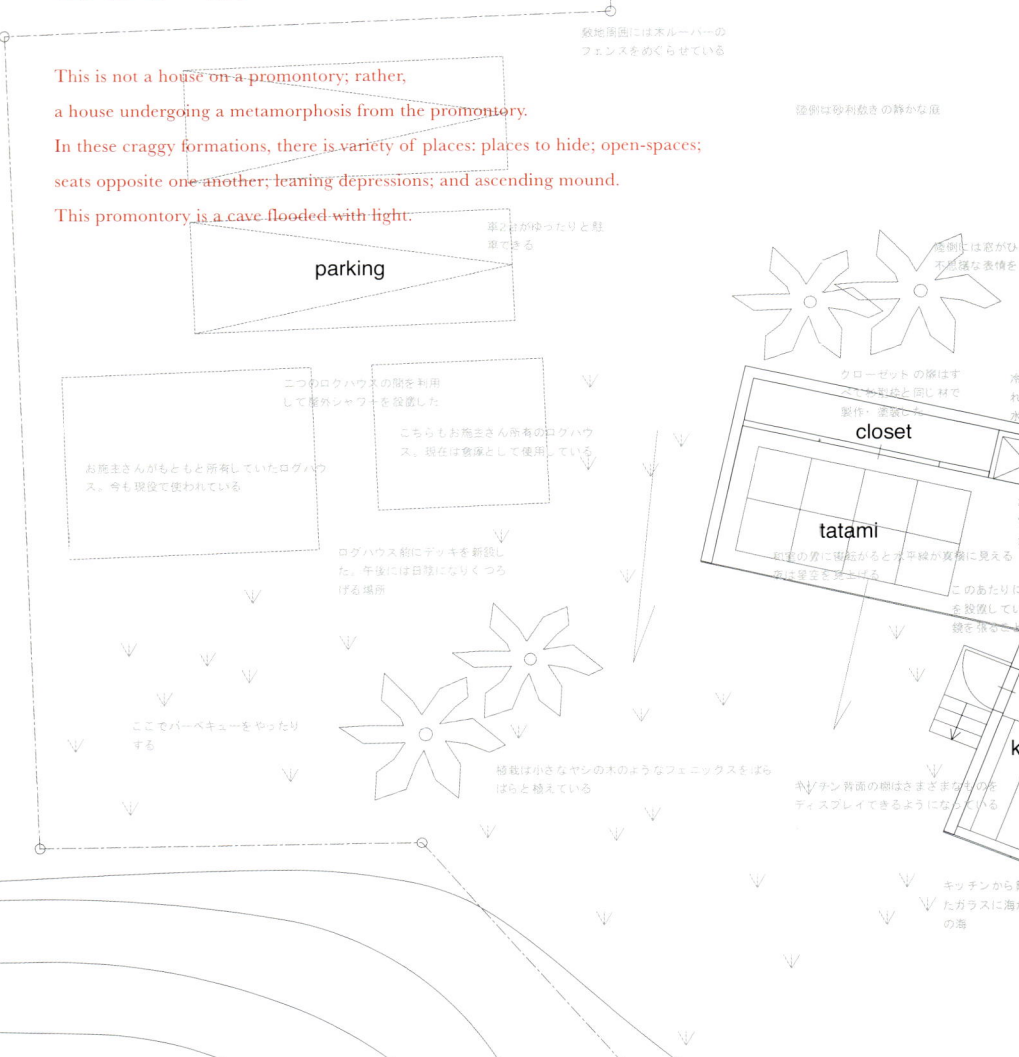

This is not a house on a promontory; rather,
a house undergoing a metamorphosis from the promontory.
In these craggy formations, there is variety of places: places to hide; open-spaces;
seats opposite one another; leaning depressions; and ascending mound.
This promontory is a cave flooded with light.

parking

closet

tatami

House O

敷地周囲には木ルーバーの
フェンスをめぐらせている

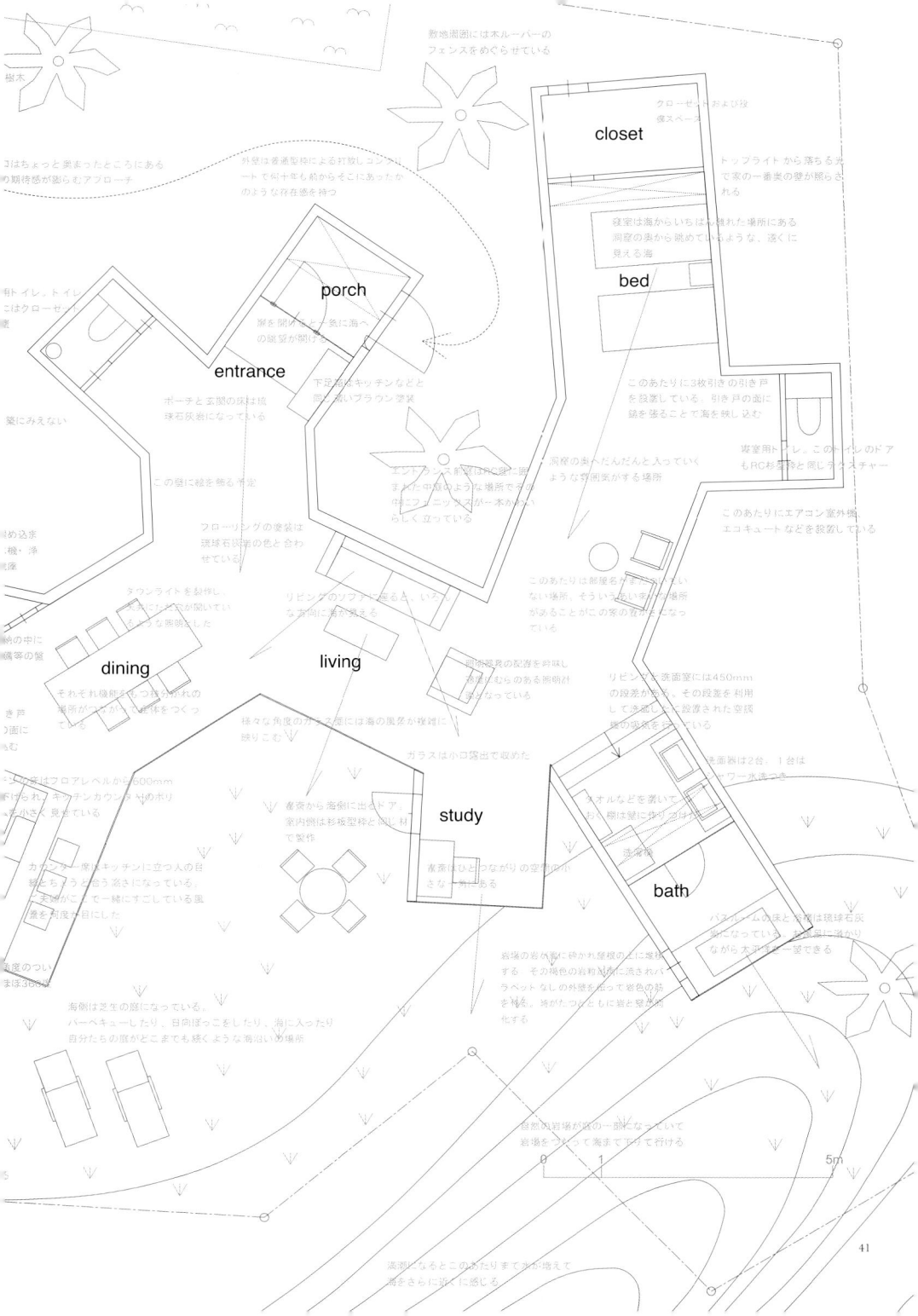

closet

クローゼットおよび設
備スペース

トップライト から落ちる光
で家の一番奥の壁が照らさ
れる

外壁は普通型枠による打放しコンクリー
トで何十年も前からそこにあったか
のような存在感を持つ

寝室は海からいちばん離れた場所にある
洞窟の奥から眺めているような、遠くに
見える海

bed

3はちょっと奥まったところにある
期待感が膨らむアプローチ

porch

樹木

このあたりに3枚引きの引き戸
を設置している。引き戸の面に
鏡を張ることで海を映し込む

用トイレ、トイレ
こはクローゼ

扉を閉めると海へ
の視界が開ける

寝室用トイレ。このトイレのドア
もRC杉型枠と同じテクスチャー

entrance

下足箱はキッチンなどと
同じ濃いブラウン塗装

ポーチと玄関の床は琉
球石灰岩になっている

築にみえない

この壁に絵を飾る予定

このあたりにエアコン室外機、
エコキュート などを設置している

エントランス側正面に近くに開
まめ、中庭のような場所で南国
中にフェニックスが一本わり
らしく立っている

このあたりは部屋名の付いてい
ない場所、そういうあいまいな場所
があることがこの家の特徴になっ
ている

フローリングの塗装は
琉球石灰岩の色と合わ
せている

タウンライトを製作し、
んで会いてい
な配置にした

リビングと洗面室には450mm
の段差があり、その段差を利用
して造られた造設された変質
熱の効果を出している

照明器具の配置を吟味し
むらのある照明計
なっている

dining

living

それぞれ様相をもつ5つの
場所がひとつの立体をつくっ
ている

bath

洗面器は2台。1台は
ャワー水治に

様々な角度のガラス戸には海の風景が複雑に
映りこむ

タオルなどを置いて
棚は壁に作りつけ

は戸
閉面
にて

ガラスは小口露出で収めた

洗濯機

書斎から海側に出るドア。
室内側は杉型枠と同じ材
で製作

study

はフロアレベルが+600mm
なり、キッチンカウンタまでの
ッ小さく見えている

書斎はひとつながりの空間の中
の一隅である

バスルームの床と浴槽は琉球石灰
岩になっている
ながら太平洋を一望できる

カウンター側キッチンに立つ人の目
線とちょうど合うような窓になっている。
主婦が家庭で一緒にすごしている風
景を重度と大切にした

浴場の岩外壁に砕かれた壁板の上に塗装
する。その褐色の岩板が雨に流されパ
ラペット なしの外観を使って岩色の筋
を残す。時がたつとともに通を重ねか
化する

度のつい
まほ365

海側は芝生の庭になっている。
バーベキューをしたり、日向ぼっこをしたり、海に入ったり
自分たちの庭がどこまでも続く ような海沿いの場所

自然の岩場が庭の一部になっていて
岩場をつたって海まで下りて行ける

0 1   5m

渇潮になるとこのあたりまで水が増えて
海をさらに近くに感じる

Diagonal Walls/Group Home in Noboribetsu, 2006

壁であり、壁でない。つながっていて同時に離れている。
壁であることと、壁でないことが連続的に変化する。

A wall and yet not a wall. Connected and simultaneously disengaged.
The condition of being a wall and not being a wall alternates in reciprocal transformation.

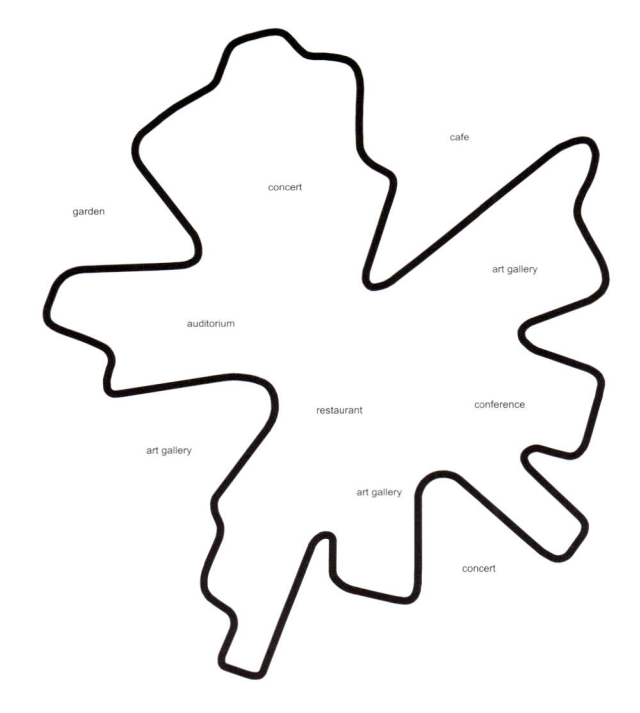

1本の線でできた一番単純な建築プラン。多様な関係性の場。

A very simple architectural plan is created by a single line. A place of manifold interactions.

Annaka Art Forum, project, 2003

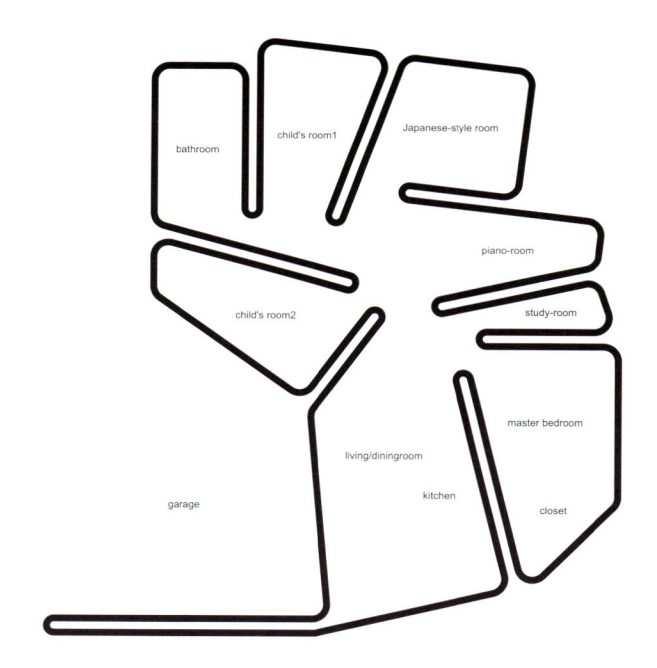

離れていて同時につながっている。すべての部屋が相互に依存しあっている。

Spaces are separated and connected at the same time. All rooms are interdependent.

T House, 2005

さまざまな人がさまざまなことをしながらも共有できる、
ひとつの広場のような空間。無関係なものたちが共存し、相互に刺激しあう場。

Like an urban square in which various people can partake in various events and still be sharing a singular space. A place where unrelated things can coexist and interdependently stimulate one another.

Annaka Art Forum

約 90 ㎡という限られた広さのなかの空間の無限の関係性。
一歩歩を進めるごとに、家のなかの風景が再編され、新しい風景が立ち現われる。

Infinite spatial interactions were realized within the finite dimension of 90m².
With every step, interior view of the house transforms and new scenery appears.

T House

4 街であり、同時に家であるような
City as House - House as City

東京とは、都市であると同時に、それ自体がどこか家のような場所である。
曲がりくねった街路の雑多で小さなスケール。
木造の小さな家々に取り囲まれた街路はもうひとつの生活空間である。
精神病院の設計をいくつか行なった。
そこでは家の快適さと都市的な多様さという根源的な両義性が求められる。
例えば生活空間があいまいに外延してできたような小さな街や、
複雑な街路空間としてのパサージュは、
家と都市が入れ子になったかのような心地のよい空間だ。
部分への微視的視線があまり意味をもたない、複雑な関係性が織り成すプリミティヴな全体。
住むことの複雑さを機能によって固着化せず、複雑なままに建築化することは可能だろうか。
そのとき建築は、都市であり同時に家であるような、
そして都市でもなく家でもない新しい存在だといっていい。

Tokyo is a city and equally a place like someone's home. The city is animated by motley of winding streets of small scales. Streets aligned with small, wooden houses comprise a different type of domestic space. I have designed numerous psychiatric centers whose programs necessitated the duality of a residential comfortability and a city-like multiplicity. For example, some small cities have developed as an erratic extension of a domestic space or passages that manifested into complex streetscapes and produced delightful spaces as if a city and a house became nested within each-other. Microscopic analysis of a fraction is meaningless against this primitive totality of sophisticated interdependencies.

Can architectural expressions uphold the intricacies of daily-lives instead of conforming to the rules of functionalism? There will be a new emergence of architecture at the moment when a city becomes a house, and simultaneously neither a city nor a house.

Children's Center for Psychiatric Rehabilitation, 2006

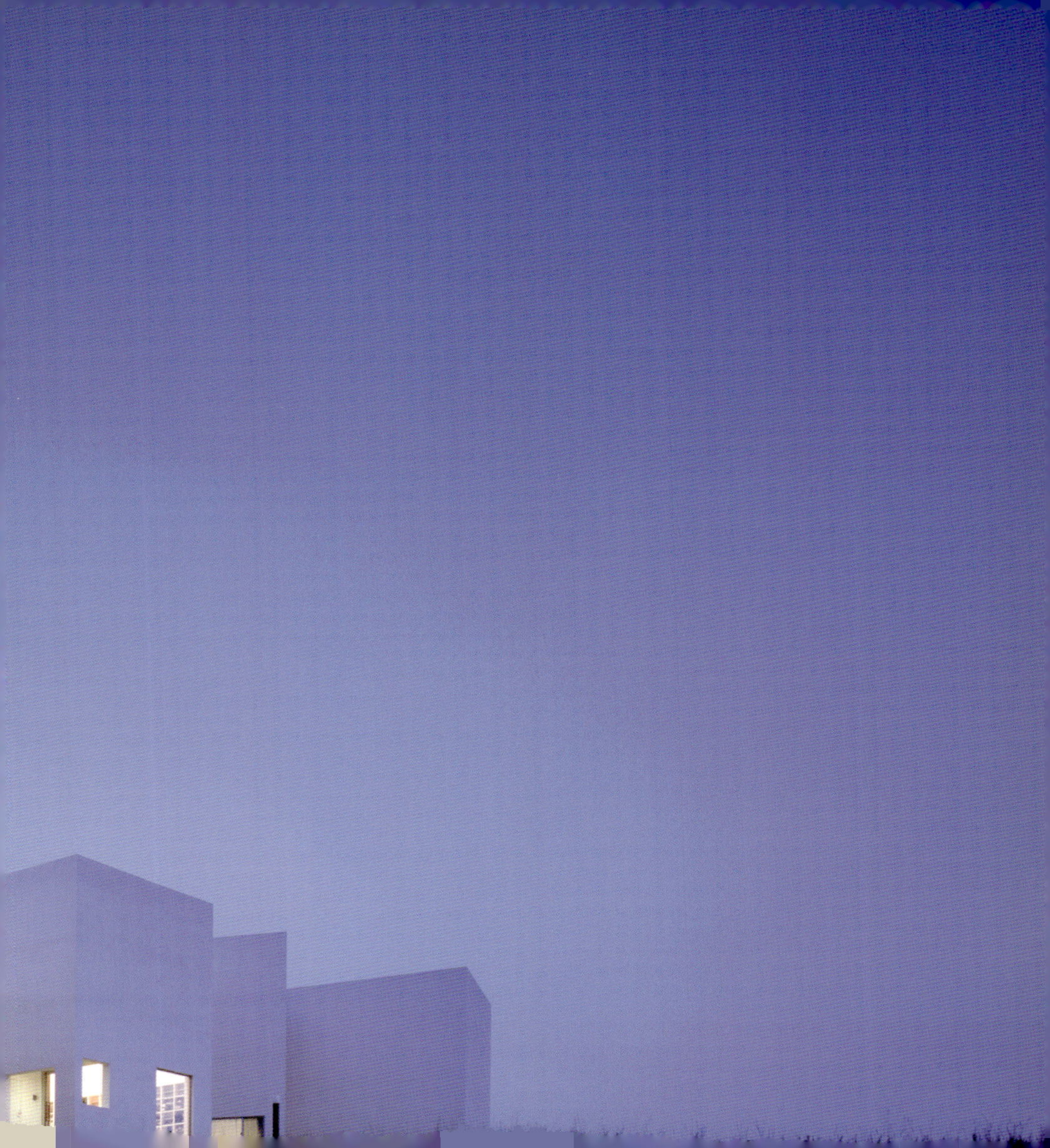

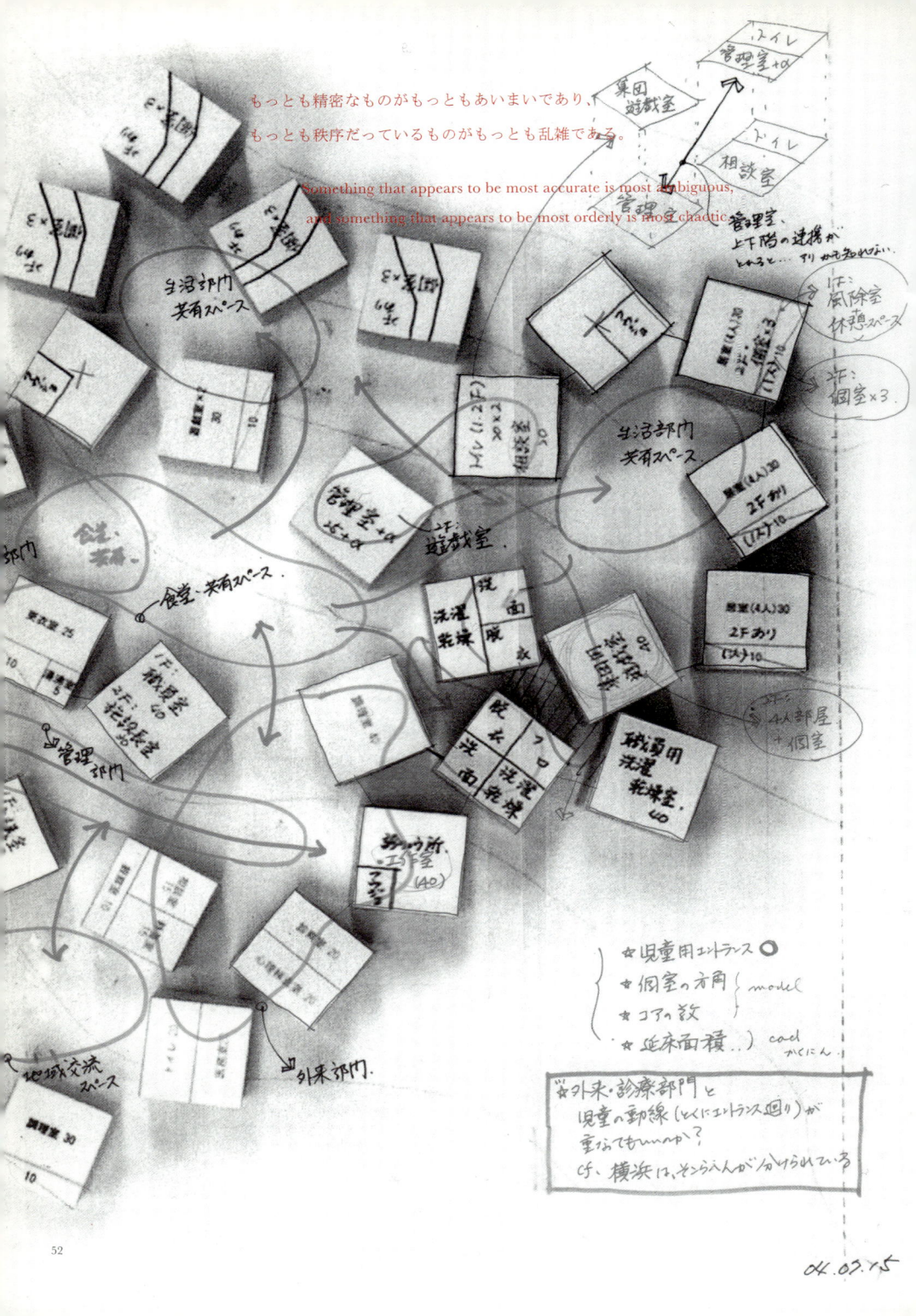

もっとも精密なものがもっともあいまいであり、
もっとも秩序だっているものがもっとも乱雑である。

Something that appears to be most accurate is most ambiguous,
and something that appears to be most orderly is most chaotic.

どこまでも精密に設計していく。どこまでも偶然性が残り続ける。

Strenuously designed with precision. Endless serendipities subsist.

Children's Center for Psychiatric Rehabilitation

str

waiting room

library

office

alcove

multipurpose space

court

場所を見つけだしていく。
アルコーヴ。くぼみ。幾何学的な、光に満ちた透明な洞窟。

It is to discover a place.
An alcove. An indentation. A geometrical, transparent cave infused with light.

kitchen

alcove

staff room

alcove

living area 1

br

alcove

br

br

0 5m

Children's Center for Psychiatric Rehabilitation

この平面は、小さな集落のようでもあり、原子的な生物のようでもあり、
たんぱく質分子のようでもあり、数学の公式のようでもあり、
象形文字のようでもあり、開放性と閉鎖性の同居でもあり……
つまり複雑さと秩序の準安定な均衡である。

This plan emulates small villages, atomistic organisms, protein molecules,
mathematical formulae, ideographs, and embodies the dichotomy of openness and seclusion;
simply put, it is in a metastable equilibrium between pandemonium and order.

Rehabilitation Dormitory in Hokkaido, 2003

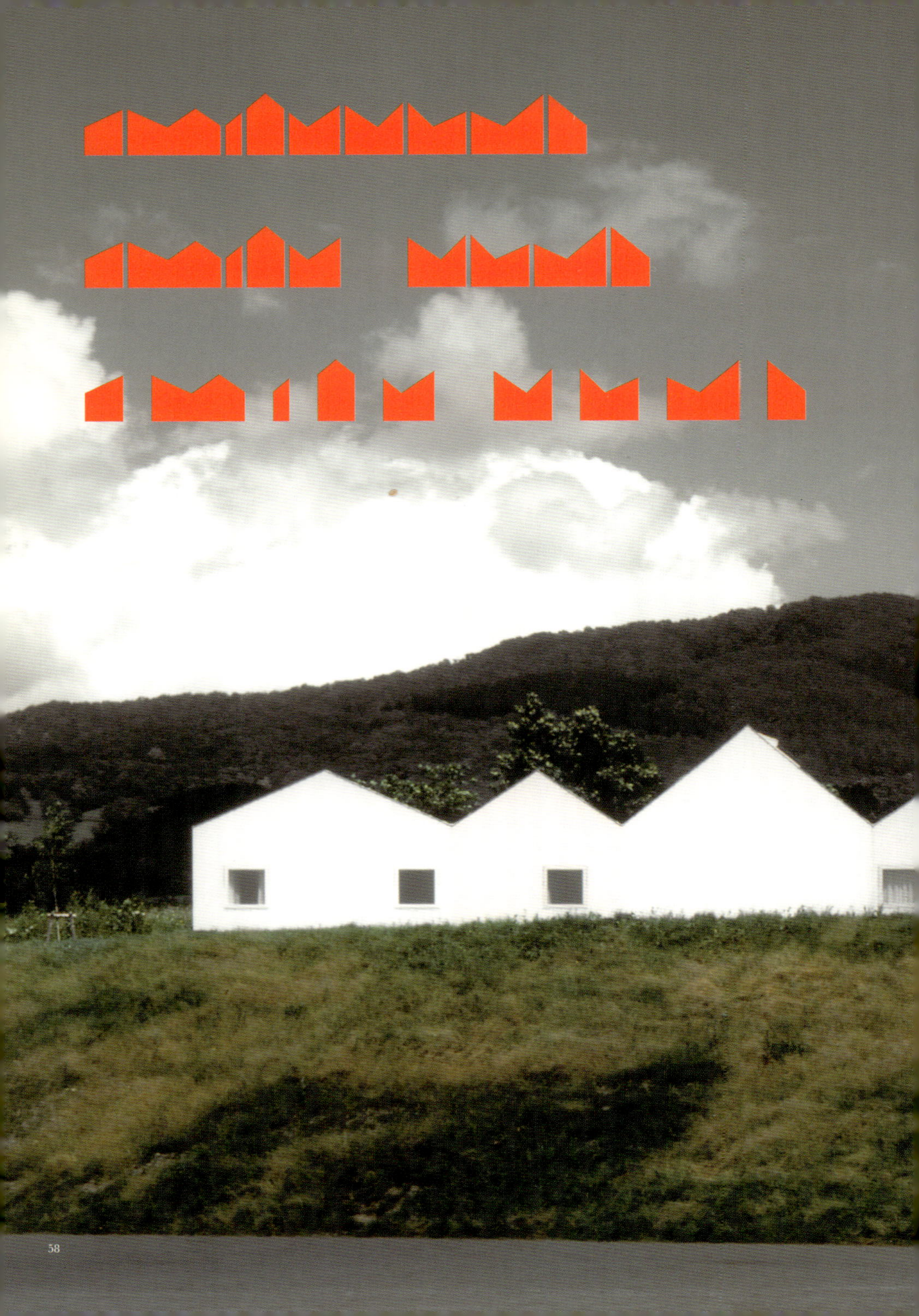

2つの住宅、7つの家型、9つの部屋。
それらの重なりのずれのなかに、空間が現われる。

Two houses, seven house-forms, nine rooms.
Spaces emerge within the overlapping slippages.

7/2 House, 2006

森と同じ作られ方で建築を作ることはできないだろうか。

Can architecture develop analogously to the way forests do?

Aomori Prefectural Art Museum, 2000

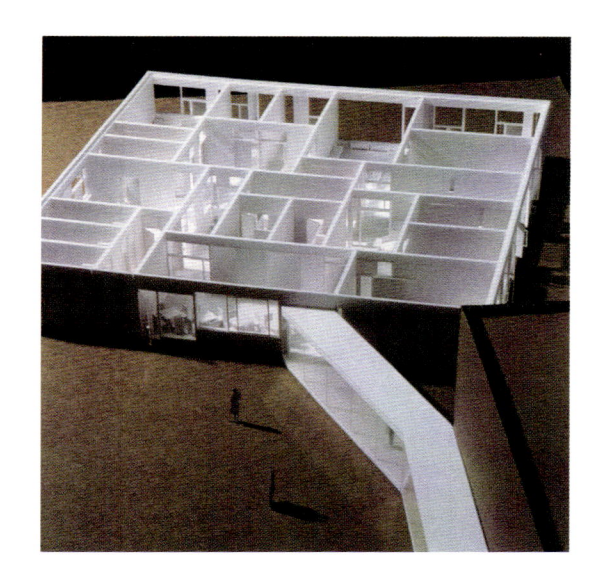

廊下のない建築。部屋が細胞のように寄り添っている。

Architecture without corridors. Rooms are shearing like cellular tissues.

Seidai Hospital Annex, 1999

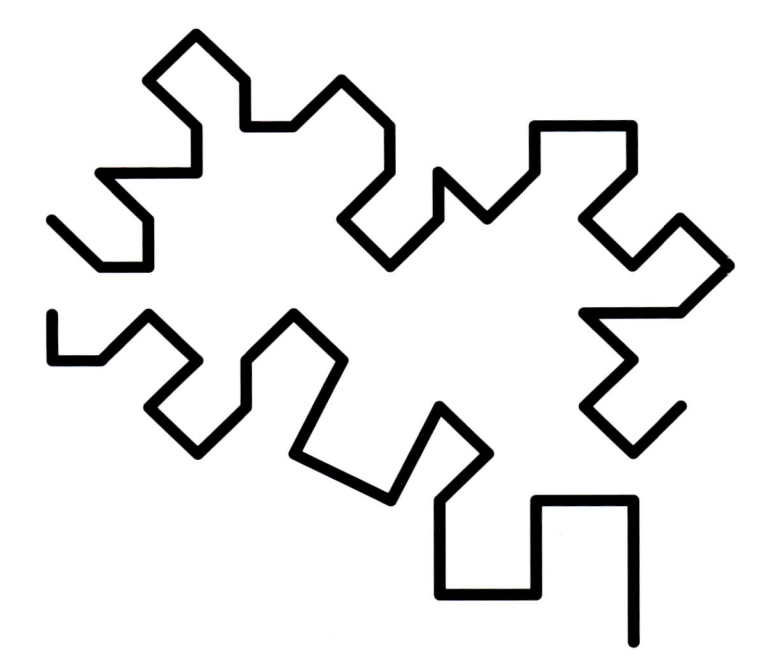

人工物と自然物のあいだ。

Geometry between artificial and natural.

Aomori Art Museum

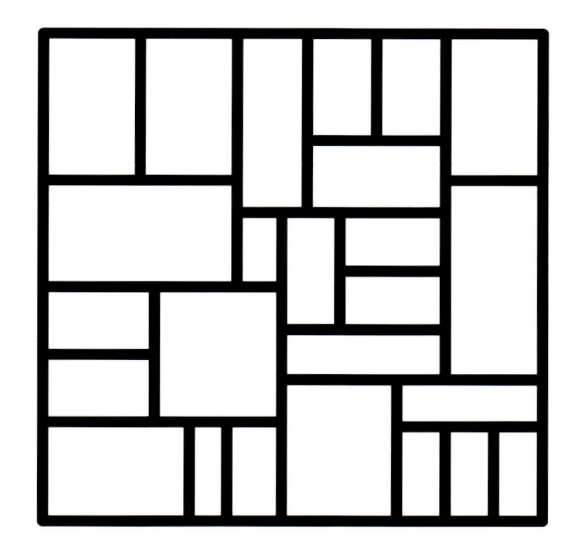

部分というのは単位ではない。全体がなくなったら部分もなくなる。
部分がなくなったら全体もなくなる。未分化な場のネットワーク。

To be a part does not equate to being a unit. If the whole is gone, so will the parts.
If a part is gone, so will the whole. Network of an emergent field.

Seidai Hospital Annex

5 大きな樹のなかに住むような
In a Tree-like Place

House Inside-Out Tree, 2007

家に住むということは、大きな樹のなかに住むことに似ている。いくつもの枝があって、それぞれの枝はそれぞれ快適な居場所となっている。完結した部屋ではなく、関係しあう居場所。
ある枝から別の枝が見えたり、少し隠れたり、よじ登ったりする。樹状の形よりも、居場所の立体的なネットワークの豊かさが、住むための場所の始まりを予感させる。
関係性でできた全体。樹や森の属性を考えてみる。枝は互いに方向を変えて成長し、森は自然選択的な密度とネットワークを成す。僕は「居場所」の成り立ちを、局所的な部分の集合としての全体である樹や森の成り立ちに近いものと考えている。自然そのものではなく、乱雑さと不確定性を孕んだ空間、樹や森と同じ「質」を、新しい座標系とともに発見すること。

To live in a house is akin to living in a tree.
There are many branches and each is a pleasant place to be. They are not hermitically isolated rooms, but connected and continually redefining each-other. From one's respective positions as one climbs this proverbial tree, another branch may appear or may fade away from view. The variegated three-dimensional network of localities foreshadows a new conception of domestic place.
Totality formed by interrelationships. Take the evolution of trees and forests. Branches develop while reciprocally altering its own directionality; forests survive by networks and densities resulting from natural selection. The evolution of "place-making" can be comparable to the growth of forests and trees, whose overall scheme is agglomerate set of foci.
People can discover a new coordinate system with a space impregnated by chaotic and uncertain elements analogous to, though not to purely imitate, trees and forests.

House Inside-Out Tree

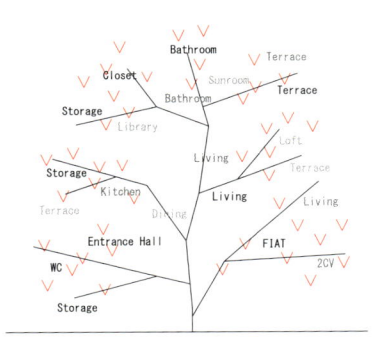

それぞれの枝にはそれぞれの居場所があり、さまざまに関係しあっている。

Each branch is a unique place and yet interrelates with each other.

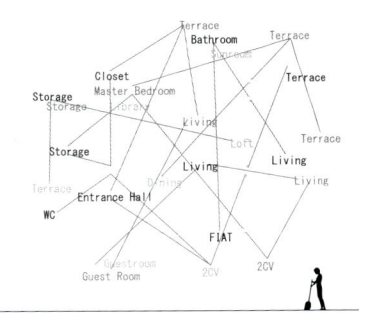

枝の構造ではなく、その関係のネットワークだけを取り出して空間化する。

Find spatial expressions in the network of interactions rather than in the structure of branches.

浮遊するたくさんの小さなスラブ。
枝から枝へと飛び移るような、身体的な住処。

Numerous small hovering slabs. They compose corporeal spaces for jumping from branches to branches.

House NA, 2007

通常の階高の半分の高さの空間を積み上げて作ったアトリエ。
半分は人間に合っていて、半分は人間にとって他者であるような空間。

着物と、人との間のずれ。
ずれ自体が、姿となる。ずれ自体が、構造になる。形式になる。

Atelier/House in Hokkaido, 2005-

Atelier accumulated from spaces half the conventional height of floors.
Half-ness is scaled for humans, and half-ness is an indifferent space.

A gap between clothing and person. The gap itself constitutes a figure.
The gap itself constitutes a structure. It becomes a form.

床も壁も天井も、すべてに大きな穴が開いている。遺跡のなかに住んでいるような家。

Floors, walls and ceilings are all punctuated by large holes. It is a house, but like living in a ruin.

House H, 2007-

6 あいまいな領域のなかに住む
Nebulous

建築というのは、その始まりにさかのぼって考えると、
さまざまな密度の濃淡による「ぼんやりとした領域」なのではないだろうか。
内と外とは、場の密度の違いに過ぎない。家と街は、同じものの違った現われとなる。
「家」と「街」、「内」と「外」、「虚の空間」と「実の空間」などを2つの独立した対概念と考えずに、
「家かつ街」「内かつ外」「虚かつ実の空間」という関係性は可能か、と捉え直してみる。
すると、2つのあいだの領域は溶解して入れ子状になりながら、無限の階調に色づくだろう。
無限の階調は、限りなく「街」に近い「家」、「内」が限りなく外延してできた「外」など、
新しいさまざまな姿をして現われる。
ぼんやりしたこの領域は、全体性や大きな秩序への指向をもたない、距離感と関係性の場である。

When one thinks of architecture's origin,
one can imagine it to be a "nebulous field" derived from various densities of chiaroscuros.
Whether to be inside or outside was entirely contingent upon the differences in local densities.
A house and a city can be thought of as differentiated phenomena, both from a singular condition.
Rather than thinking in terms of two dialectical oppositions in the likes of "house" versus "city,"
"inside" versus "outside" and "implied space" versus "absolute space,"
it is possible to reformulate the relationship as "a house and a city," "inside and outside"
and "implied space and absolute space," respectively. Thus,
the unlimited gradations emerge while boundaries among elements begin to dissolve and stratify.
Infinite variables inform new conditions such as "a house acquiring resemblance of a city"
or "exteriority produced from an infinite extension of interiority."
Field of distances and interactions emerges from nebulous conditions
and refuses any predilection to totalizing systems or all-encompassing order.

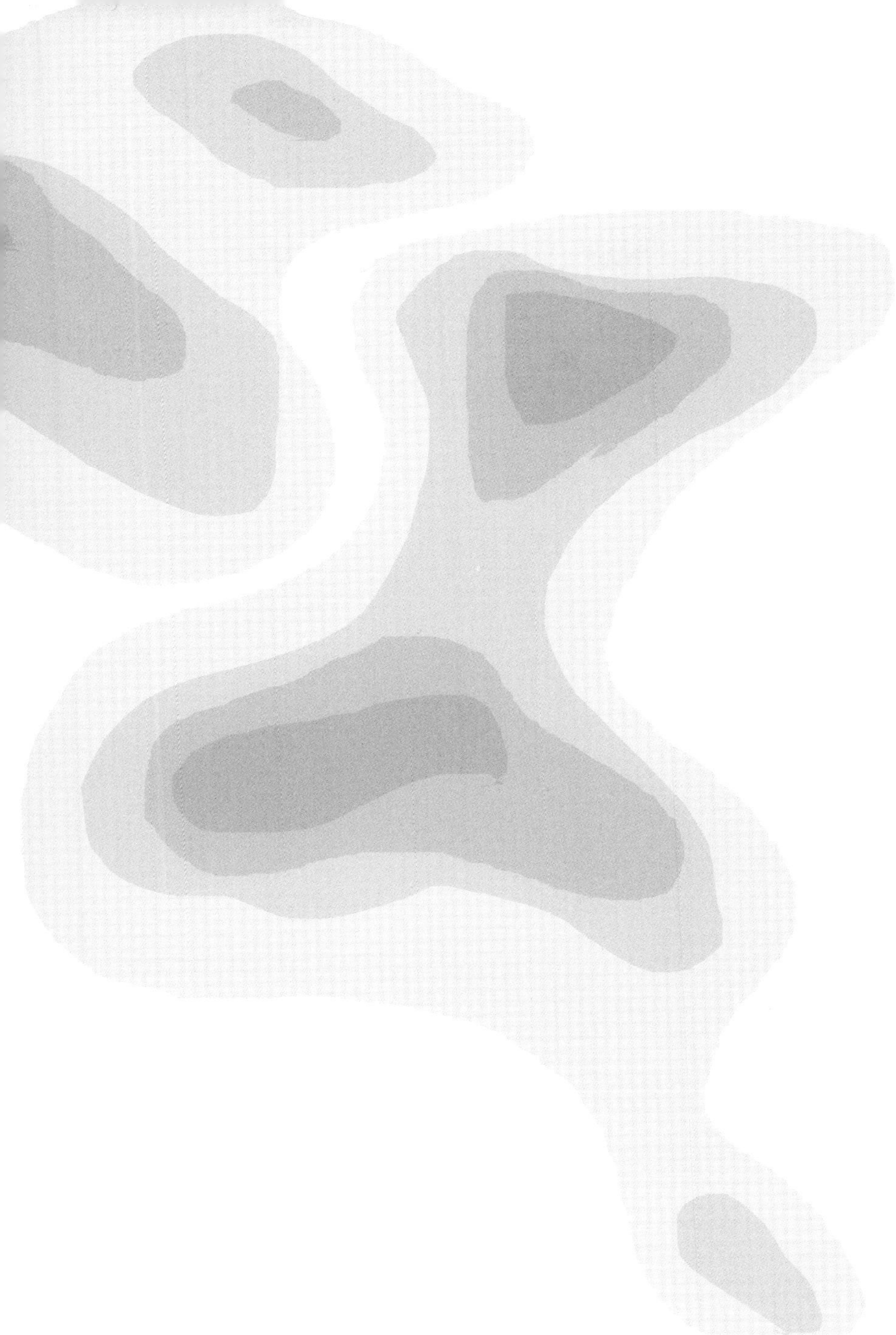

DOMESTIC ⇄ URBAN

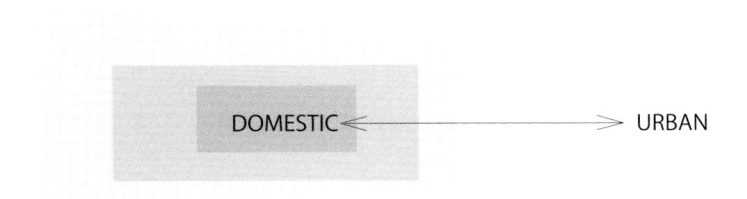

Conventional House

inside | outside

Future House!

inside & outside

内と外を分ける物体。

A construct that separates inside and outside.

都市のなかのかすかな密度の高まり。グラデーション。

Infinitesimal augmentation of urban density. Gradation.

House N, 2008

House N

外部は建築ではない。内部も建築ではない。
外部と内部がどのように接続されているか、が建築である。

Exteriority is not architecture. Interiority is not architecture.
Architecture exists in how exteriority and interiority are connected.

House N

音楽においては形式がそのまま内容である。

In music, the formula is also the content.

砂漠の真ん中に人は住めない。
純粋な空虚は、住むための場所ではない。

Humanity cannot live in the middle of a desert.
Pure emptiness is not a place for habitation.

emptiness

単なる高密度には人は住めない。
圧迫される不快な密度は住むための場所ではない。

Humanity cannot subsist in mere high-density.
Oppressive and discomforting density is
not a conducive place for habitation.

density

空虚によって密度を作り出すということ。ポジティヴな高密度。

It is to conceive of densities from nothingness. It is a rise of positive density.

density from emptiness

「空虚の小さな塊、すきまの集合体、となってしまう。
(天ぷら) 料理はここで一つの逆説的な夢、
純粋にすきまからからだけでできている事物という逆説的な夢を、
具現するものとなる。(…中略…) 完璧な周縁を持たないすきま」——ロラン・バルト『表徴の帝国』

"…se réduit à un petit bloc de vide, à une collection de jours: l'aiment rejoint
ici le rêve d'un paradoxe: celui d'un objet purement interstitiel,
[…] l'interstice sans bords pleins" —— Roland Barthes, *L'empire des signes*

ガラスの雲。
ぼんやりとした領域のなかに住む。

Glass Cloud.
Living in an amorphous domain.

Glass Cloud, project, 2002

落ち葉が集まったように、かすかに場所の密度が作られる。
その密度の起伏を、さまざまに読み取り使いこなしていく。

A region of density faintly emerges as in the gathering of fallen foliage.
The nooks and crannies of densities are analyzed and habituated.

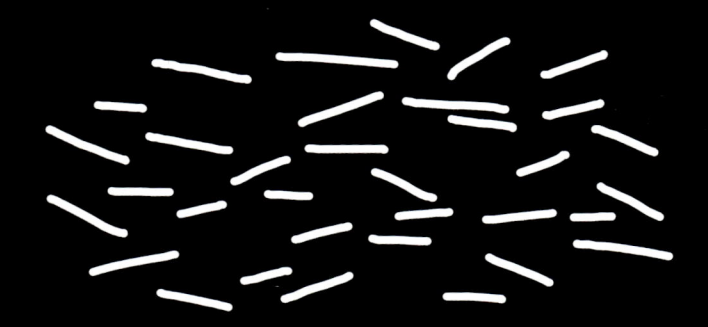

M-Hospital Day Care Center, project, 2000

Empty House, 2008-

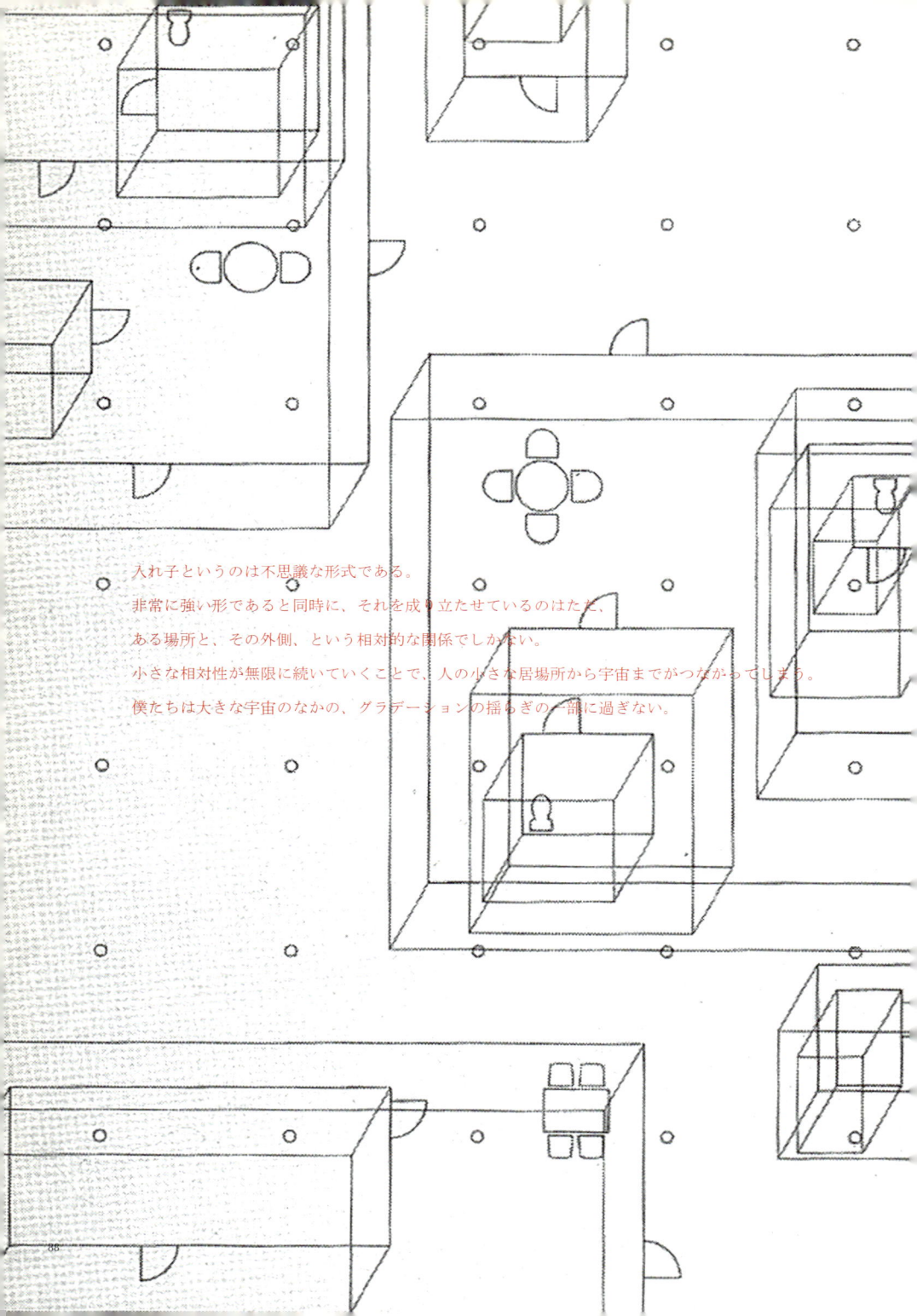

入れ子というのは不思議な形式である。
非常に強い形であると同時に、それを成り立たせているのはただ、
ある場所と、その外側、という相対的な関係でしかない。
小さな相対性が無限に続いていくことで、人の小さな居場所から宇宙までがつながってしまう。
僕たちは大きな宇宙のなかの、グラデーションの揺らぎの一部に過ぎない。

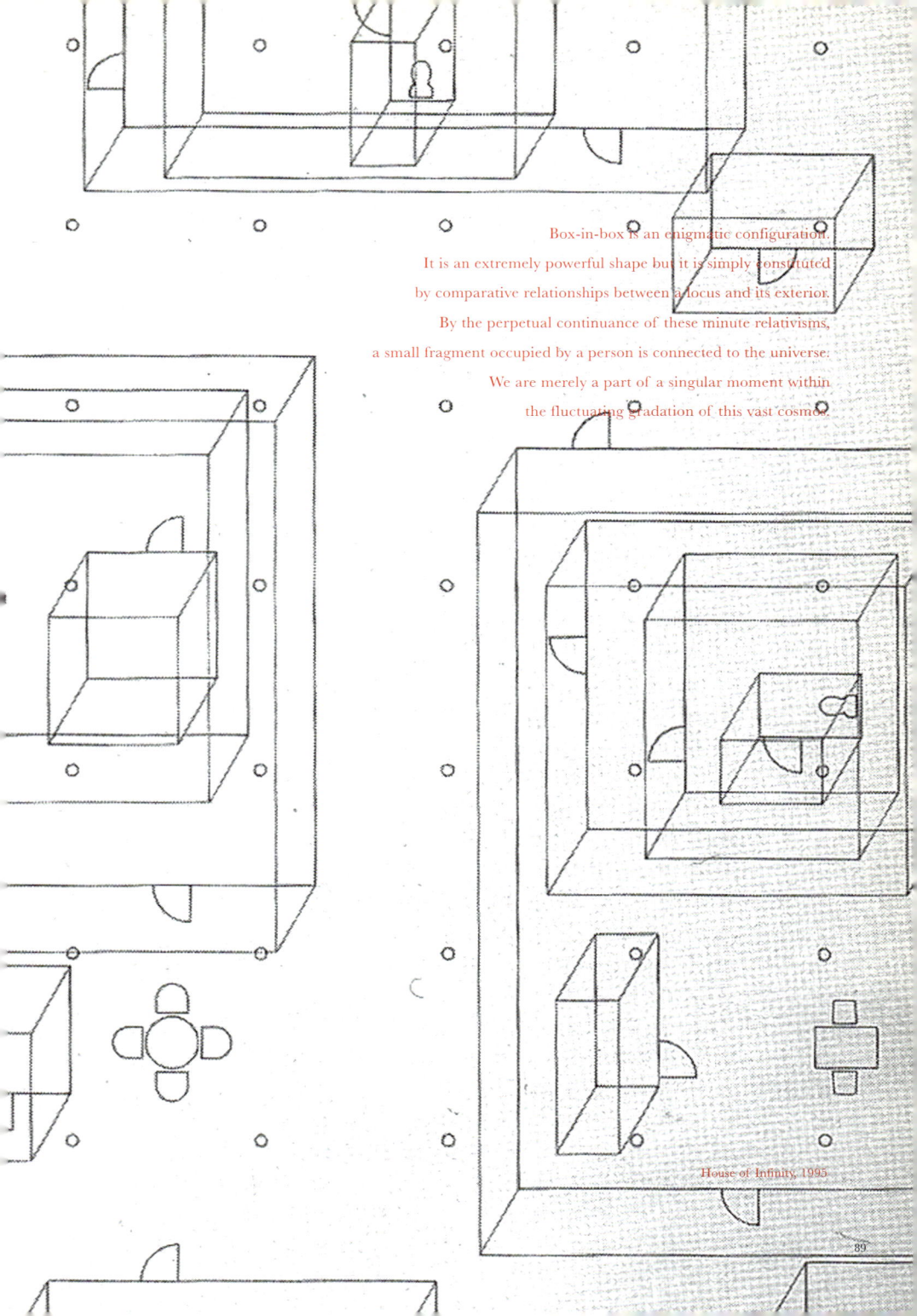

Box-in-box is an enigmatic configuration.
It is an extremely powerful shape but it is simply constituted
by comparative relationships between a locus and its exterior.
By the perpetual continuance of these minute relativisms,
a small fragment occupied by a person is connected to the universe.
We are merely a part of a singular moment within
the fluctuating gradation of this vast cosmos.

House of Infinity, 1995

7 ぐるぐる
Gūru - Gūru

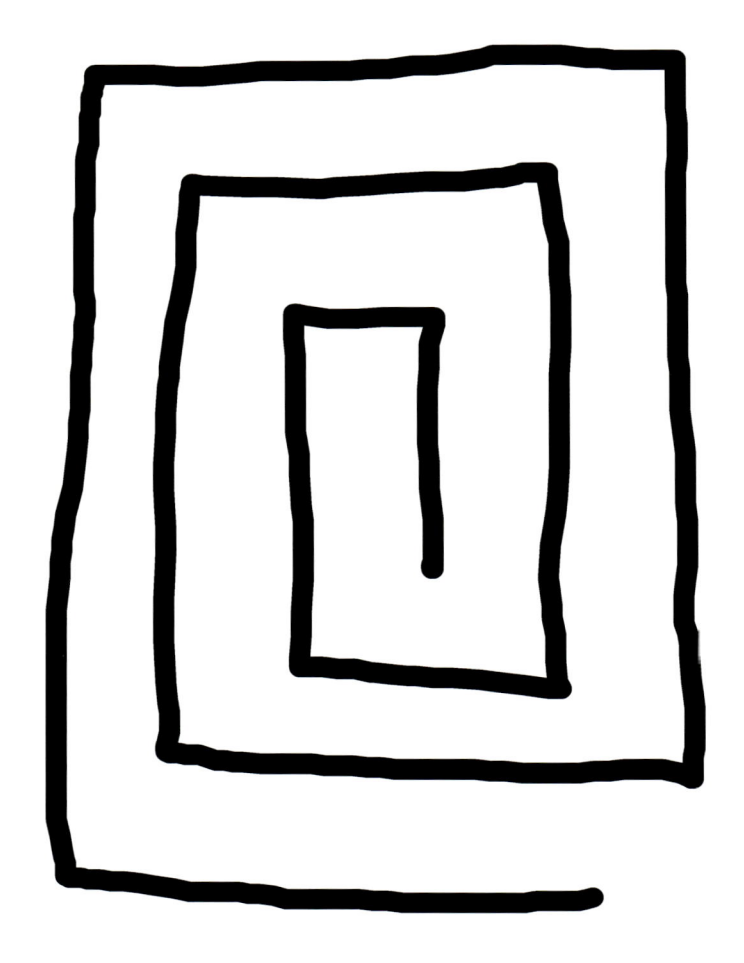

91

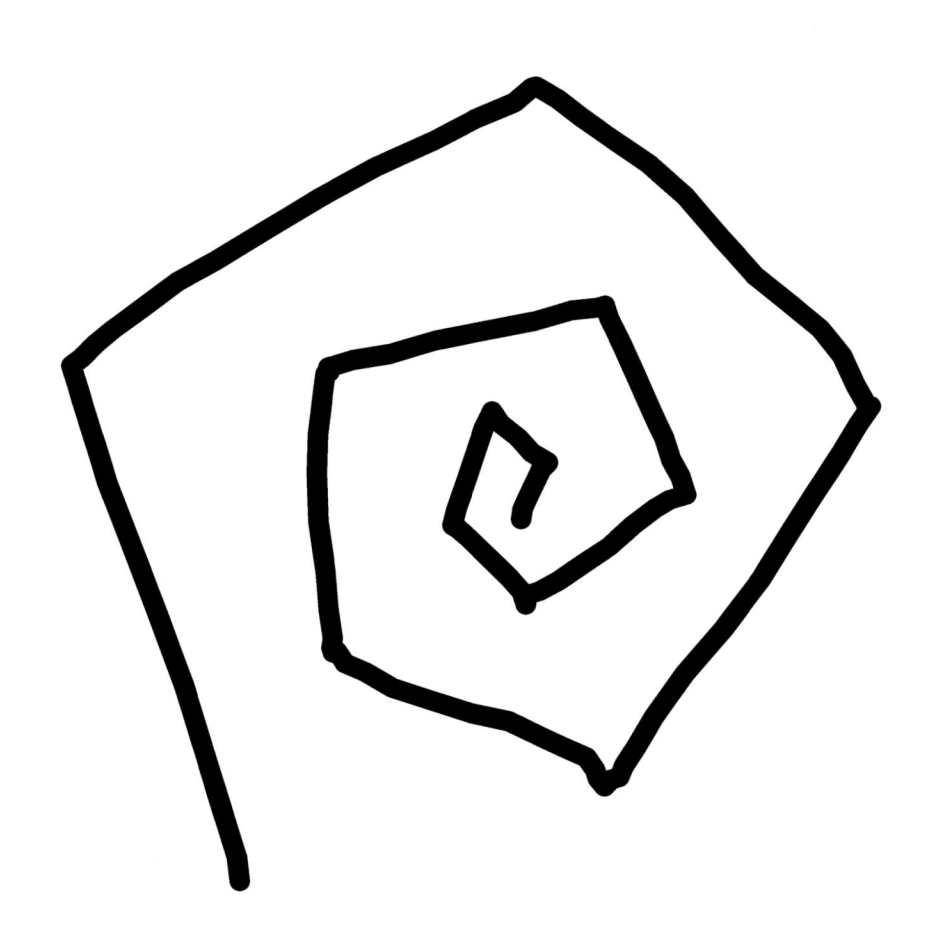

ぐるぐるとはなんだろうか。最も古い形。それでいていまだによくわからない形。すべての「外」を内化し、すべての内を外化する渦巻き。そこには無限の奥まりと無限の外延がある。連続性と断絶性が同居する。求心性と拡散性が同居する。

もしくは形態／パターンが発生するために存在した原初的時間、契機としての点。すべてを包み込んだ点を起源とする形＝ぐるぐる。それは絶対時間・均質空間を拒否し、ボルヘス「エル・アレフ」のイメージへと近接していく。

可塑的だが規定的な空間であるぐるぐるは、身体化された無限である。

What is a gürü-gürü? It is an ancient yet inexplicable form of spiral. This spiral externalizes all interiority and internalizes all exteriority. There exists infinite depths and expansion. Continuity and discontinuity coexist. Centripetal and centrifugal forces co-occur.

Perchance, it was a consequential corollary of the primordial moment that spawned morphology or patterns. Spiral forms originated as an inscription that engulfed all things. It rejects absolute time and universal space, resembling the image of *El aleph* by Jorge Luis Borges instead.

Plastic and yet concrete space of a spiral is a physicalization of infinity.

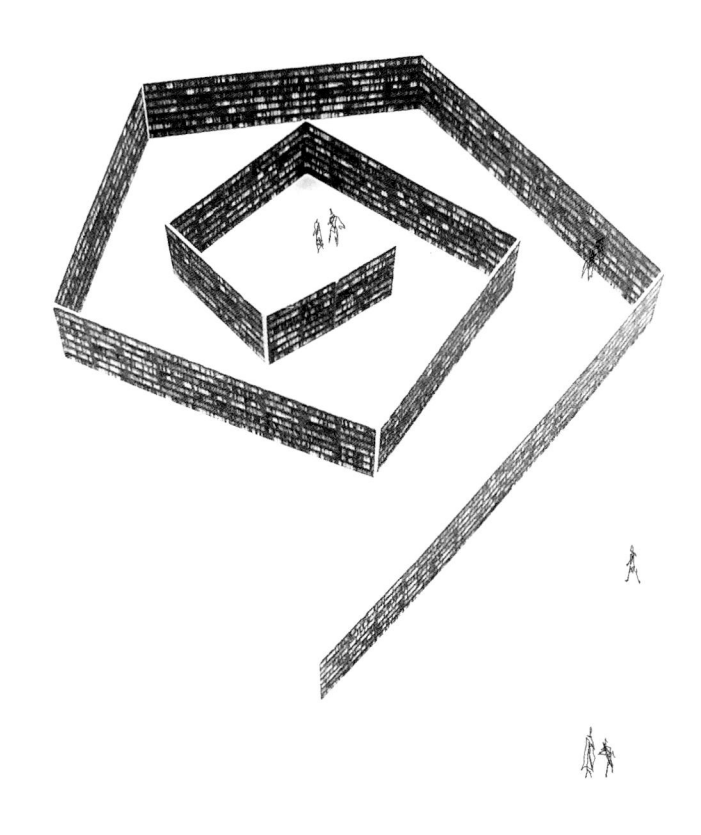

New Library and Museum of Musashino Art University, 2007-2010

図書館の計画。図書館というものの、無限性と有限性、
散策性と検索性、一覧性と個別性、秩序と無秩序、畏怖と憧れのすべてが同居する形式。
ボルヘスの図書館。

The configuration facilitates all the necessary synchronicities of infinite and finite,
browsing and referencing, totality and individuality, order and chaos,
awe and affinity inherently found in a library.
Consider the library of Borges.

New Library and Museum of Musashino Art University

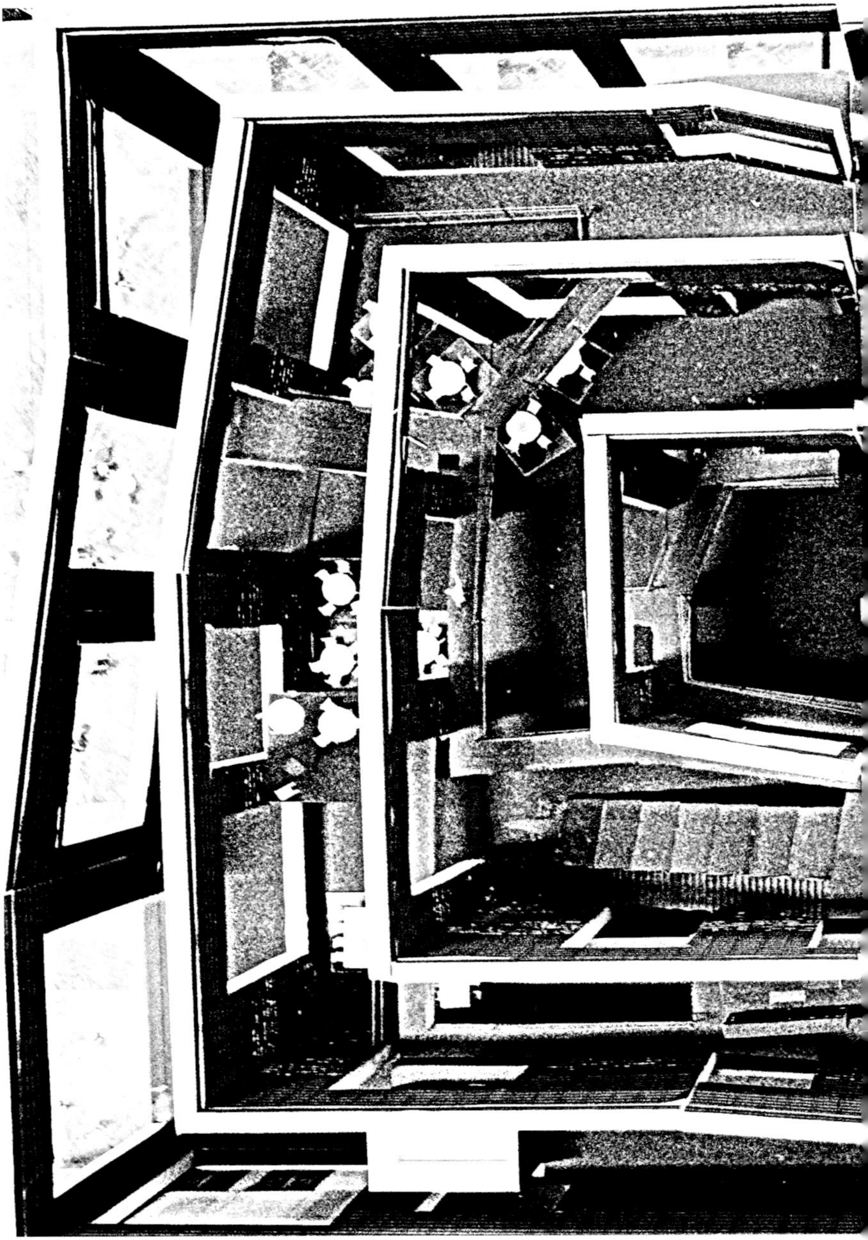

New Library and Museum of Musashino Art University

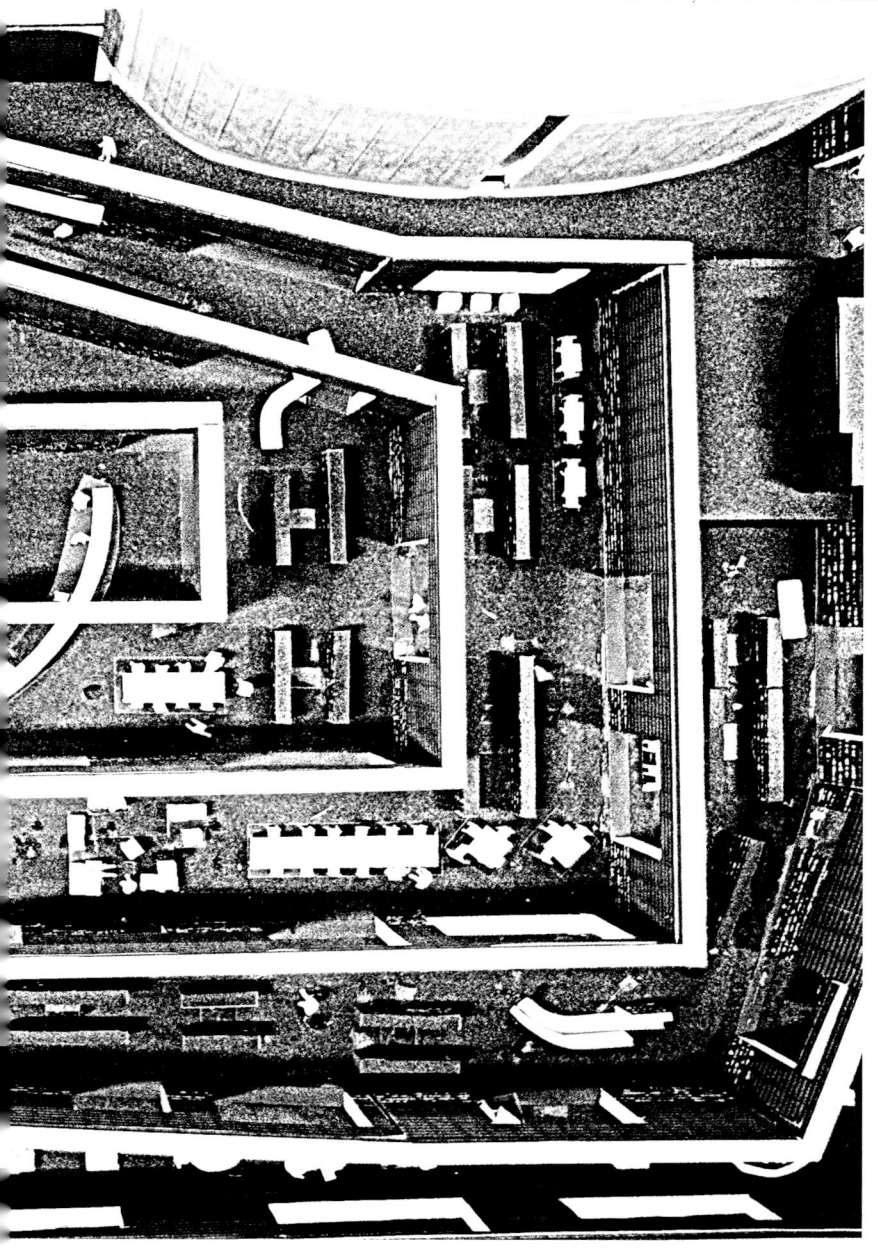

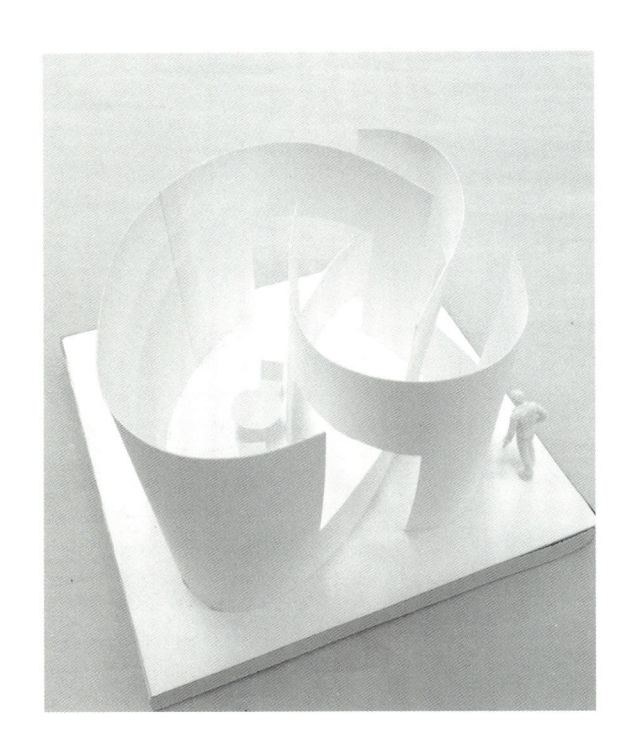

絡み合ったぐるぐる。1枚の壁によってできる無限。表と裏の絡まりあい。

An intertwining coil. Infinity transpired from a singular wall. Anteriority begins to entangle with posteriority.

House OM, 2007-

ぐるぐるの揺らぎのなかに、かすかな隅っこ＝居場所が見出される。
その隅っこを手がかりに、ぐるぐるのなかに住むための場所が生まれてくる。
ある場所の自立性と相互依存性が両立している。
広がりと落ち着きの同居。遠いところが隣にあること。

One can discover inhabitable spaces in the slight recesses
of the fluctuating spiral.
The independence and interdependence of
certain areas are mutually compatible.
Expansion and stability coexist.
Something far is actually alongside.

Spiral House, project, 2007

8 庭
Garden

ペンで敷地を囲ってみる、ペンで地形をなぞってみる。
その瞬間に建築が始まる。自然の人工化＝環境との境界形成が始まる。
だから庭は建築の原初の姿なのだ。
庭においてはすべてがあいまいである。
そこには人知を超えた無数の関係性がうごめいていて、
それぞれの関係は鮮烈であるが、総体はどこまでもあいまいなのである。
日本の回遊式庭園を歩く経験。
あいまいな境界は移動とともに、時間とともに、天気とともに揺れつづけている。
歩行とともに刻々と変化する、環境との関係的な連続性が織り込まれた経験。
あいまいな境界を空間の可能性としてとらえつづけること、
それはこれまでの建築にない豊かな経験のはずである。
建築とは屋根のかかった庭である。庭とは屋根のない建築である。

A site is encircled by a pen; landscape is traced by
a pen. Architecture began at that moment.
The artificial transformation of nature is followed by
the negotiation of its condition.
That is why a garden is the initial state of Architecture.
In a garden, everything is left indeterminate.
There persists innumerable interactions surpassing
our faculty of comprehension; each of them
spectacular yet utterly ambiguous in totality.
Such can be experienced in the perambulatory gardens of Japan.
Ambiguous boundaries pulsate with movements, time,
and weather. Continuously metamorphosing with motion,
it presents an experience inculcated by the continuity of relationships.
There must be profound experiences unseen in architecture
by seeking spatial potentials in a constant reassessment of ambiguous peripheries.
Architecture is a garden with a roof. Garden is architecture without a roof.

森のなかの住宅とは、森のなかにある場所を囲いとることだ。

A house in the forest is made from inscribing the enclosure within it.

House/Garden, 2008-

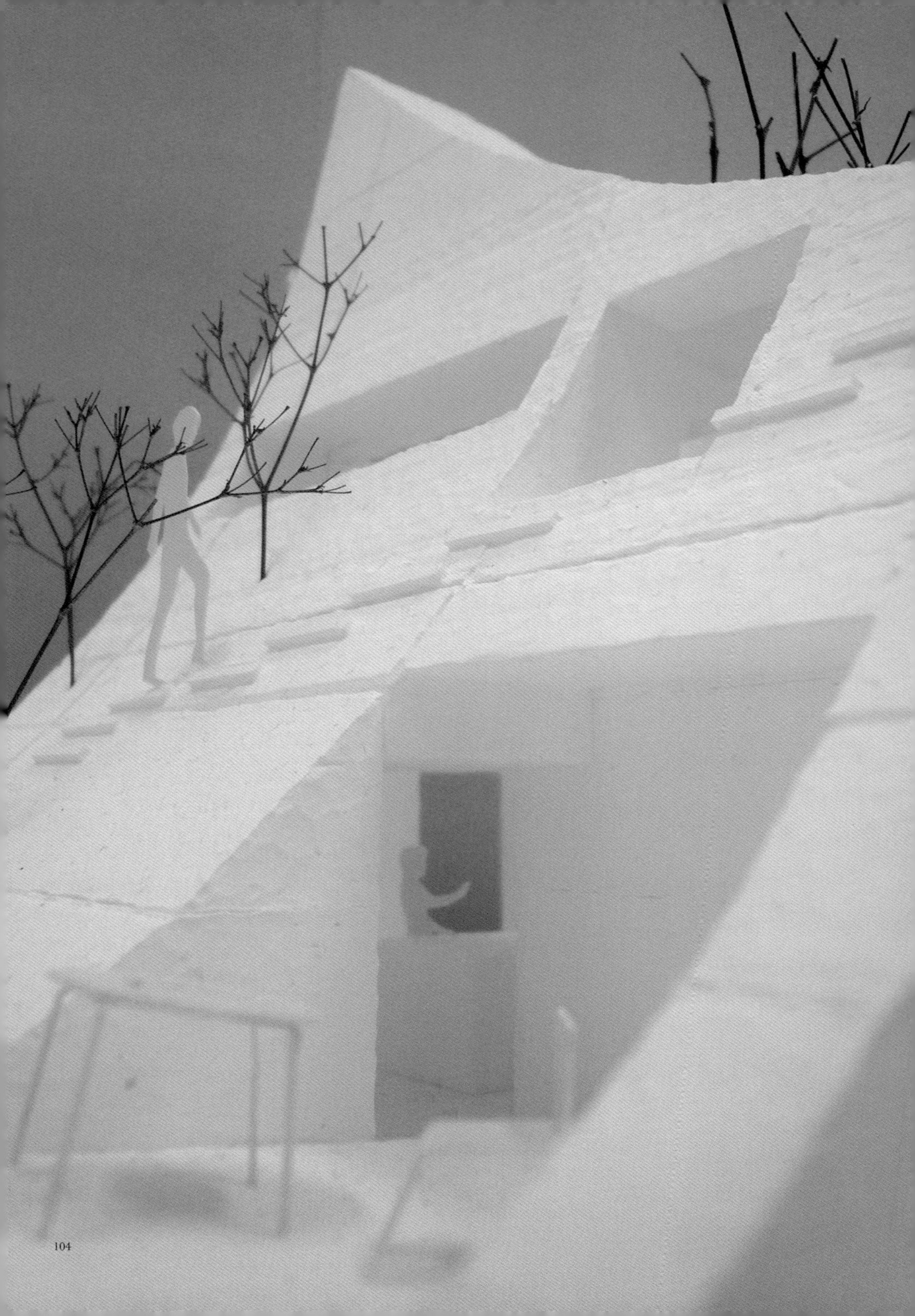

地面を歩いていると、知らないうちに壁を歩いている。
小さな山に住んでいるような。

One walks on the ground and is soon inexplicably walking on a wall.
It is as if living on a small mountain.

House I, project, 2007

家であり同時に庭である。
屋根のついた庭。外部化された建築。
庭と建築が、重なり合ってしまう。

It is a house and simultaneously a garden.
A garden with a roof. It is an externalized architecture.
Garden and architecture are superimposed.

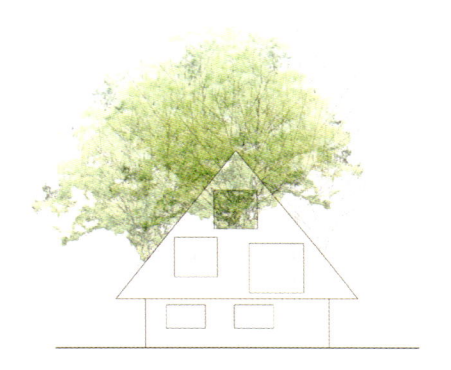

House/Forest, project, 2006

「私は庭が好きです。それは人を拒まないからです。
そこでは、人は自由に歩いたり、立ち止まったりすることができます。
庭園の全体を眺めたり、一本の樹を凝視ることができます。植物や岩や砂は、
さまざまな変化を見せています。それらはつねに変化しています」
――武満徹『音楽の余白から』

"I love gardens. It is because gardens do not reject people.
There, we can walk or stand still freely.
We can observe a garden in its entirety or stare at a single branch.
Plants and stones and sands show many changes.
They are ever-changing."
―― Takemitsu Toru, *From the Space Left in Music*

9 家と街と森が分かれる前へ
Before House and City and Forest

家とは、建築とは、人の住むための場所である。
しかし人の住むための場所は建築に限らない。
家を含みこんだ、もっと広がりのある領域のなかに人は住むのではないだろうか。
その原型にさかのぼっていくなら、家と都市とは区別されなかったに違いない。
家と森とは区別されなかったに違いない。
人間にとって未分化な状態にあった「居場所」の時点までさかのぼってみたい。
だとすれば、家であり同時に都市であり、
そして同時に森であるような場所を作り出すことができないだろうか。
それは小さな地球のような場所である。
そしてもっともプリミティヴで、もっとも未来的な建築である。

A house and the architecture as a whole, is a place for humanity.
However, a place for living is not necessarily architecture.
A person lives within a larger, expansive context that includes the notion of house.
When traced back to their origins, houses and cities must have been indistinguishable just as how
at one point houses and forests must have been indistinguishable.
Let us trace back to the moment when a human's "place to be" was
 yet in the undifferentiated state.
Then, it will be possible to envision a place that is at the same time a house,
 a city and a forest. It is a place like a small Earth.
 It would the most primitive and the most futuristic architecture.

街木住

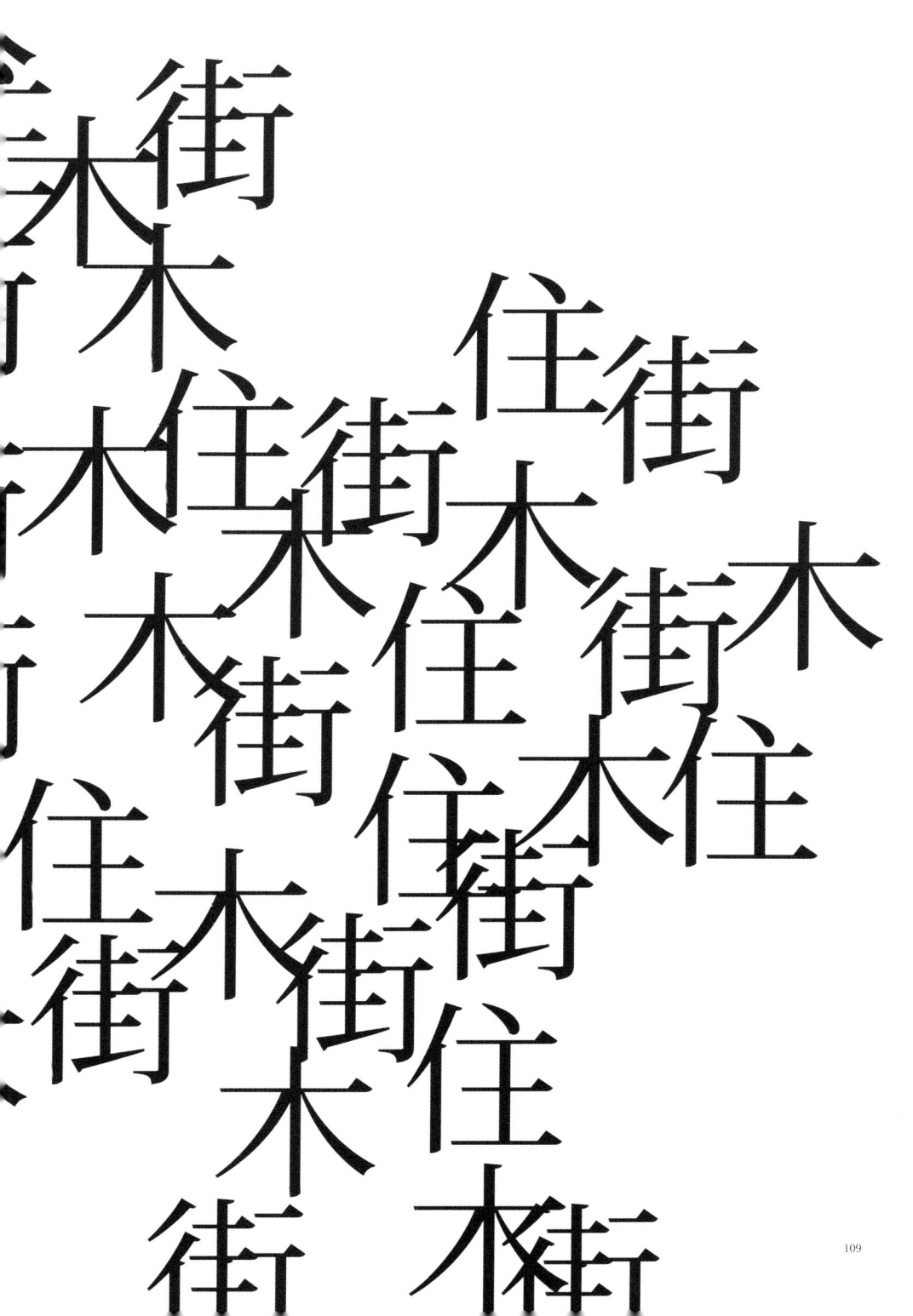

世界は物質によってではなく、対称性によってできている。

World is not made from matter, it is made from dualities.

"House before House", SUMIKA project by Tokyo Gas, 2007-2008

もっとも東京らしくて、そしてけっして存在しなかった東京。

Most-like Tokyo, and yet, a Tokyo that could have never existed.

Tokyo Apartment, 2006-2009

最小限の小さな箱＝部屋の上に、大きな樹が生えている。
この樹が生えた箱をでたらめに積み上げていくと、
穴だらけの小さな山のような、
あるいは自然発生的に生まれた集落のような場ができあがる。
住むということのさまざまなつまらなくも貴重な総体を、
ひとつの家の新しい形のなかに解き放ちたいと思う。

A large tree grows on top of the smallest possible box, a room.
By nonsensically stacking the boxes with maturing trees,
a place emerges parallel to organically developed villages
or a small mountain perforated by holes.
Within the new configuration of this house,
various trivial yet invaluable moments that constitute
our daily lives can be cherished and liberated.

"House before House"

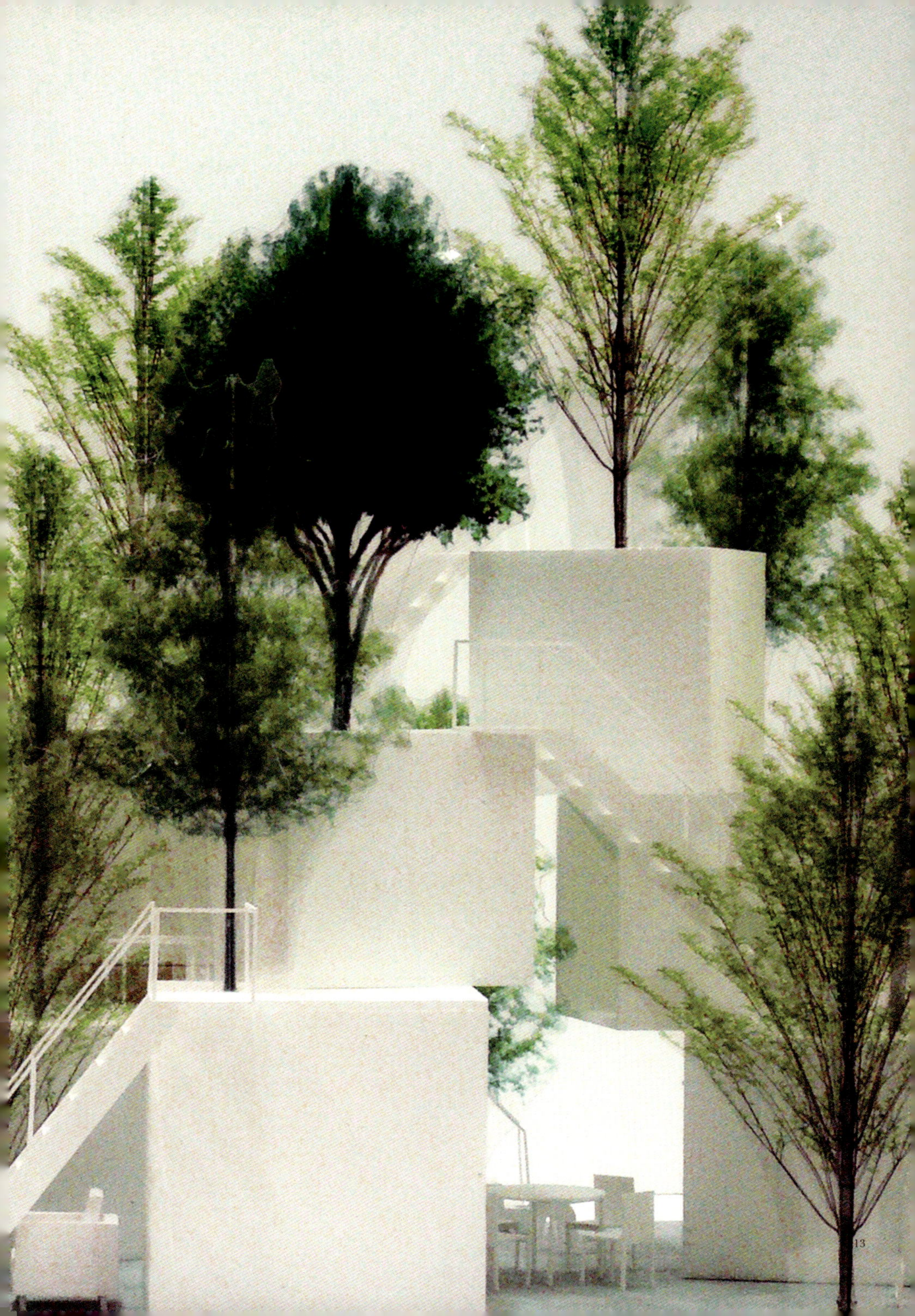

5つの住戸からなる集合住宅。
それぞれの住戸は 2-3 個の家型と、それらを結ぶ階段からなる。
つまりひとつの住戸は、居室と、その間の都市空間の両方によって成り立っている。
ほかの住戸の屋根を歩いて移動したり、家と家の隙間から思わぬ光が入ってきたり、
懐かしくも未来的な東京の姿。

It is a multifamily housing composed of five living units.
Each unit has two to three house-shaped compartments connected by stairs.
Thus, one living unit is constituted from rooms and urban spaces in between them.
This vision of Tokyo appears familiar and yet equally futuristic as light
can enter unexpectedly from between houses or one can walk on neighbors' roofs.

Tokyo Apartment

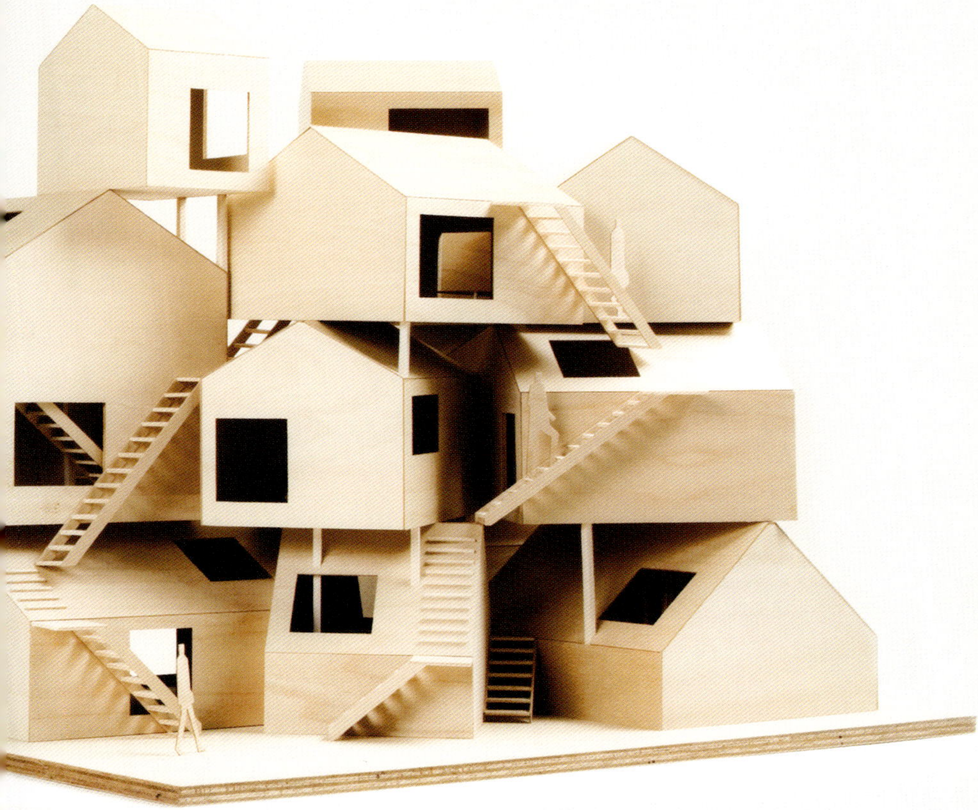

樹木の下には場ができ、人が集まって過ごす。
原始的な小さな家型の壁が、上空で細かく枝分かれして空気のヴォリュームを作る。
この家には屋根がない。あるいは厚い空気の大きな屋根がある。
草原のなかのパヴィリオン。

People gather and spend time under a tree-like place.
This structure has no roof. Instead, there is a large cover of thickened air.
A pavilion in middle of a prairie.

Between House and Tree, project, 2008

10 ものと空間が分かれる前へ
Before Matter and Space

ものと空間が分かれる前、
その圧倒的な未分化な状態が内包する無限定の可能性。
35cmのムクの角材を積み上げて作る小さな住まいのプロジェクト。
積み上げる木材とそのあいだにできる空間がほぼ等価となるとき、
ものによって空間ができるのか、空間によってものが生まれるのか、
その境目は限りなくあいまいになる。その未分化から再び建築を構想する。
未分化ゆえに、そこから場所が、住まいが、
よりどころが、都市が、統合体として生まれてくる。
建築の始まりにさかのぼる。未来の建築は同時に原初的な建築である。
ものと空間は別々のものではない。音と沈黙は別々のものではない。

Before matter and space separated,
there was an unfathomable potential concealed
in the unequivocally undifferentiated state.
A small residential project was realized from stacking rectilinear,
raw timbers in 35 cm intervals.
When the stacked timbers and interstitial spaces become equivalent,
ambiguities blur the distinction between the space
produced by mass and the mass produced by space.
Reconsider architecture from that primordial state.
Its protean nature engenders complete elements;
differentiating into fields, houses, epicenters, cities, and so on.
Retrograde to the origin of architecture.
Architecture of the future is at the same time architecture of the primordial.
Matter and space are not disparate things.
Sound and silence are not disparate things.

ものから空間が生まれ、空間からものが生まれる。

粒子と反粒子が、無から生成する。

闇のなかの影絵。

Space was born from matter, and matter was born from space.

Particles and anti-particles were created in a vacuum.

A silhouette in the darkness.

Next Generation Wooden Bungalows, 2005-2008

♩

人工の建築、自然の建築

藤森照信［ふじもり・てるのぶ／建築史・建築家］×藤本壮介

建築の虚と実、反転する建築

藤森照信　藤本さんがル・コルビュジエに関心を持っていると聞いてびっくりしたのですが、どういう部分に興味があるのですか？

藤本壮介　ル・コルビュジエは学生の時からずっと好きでした。昨年ヨーロッパに建築を見に行ったのですが、結局ル・コルビュジエ・ツアーになってしまいました。ル・コルビュジエの実物を見たのは学生時代以来約10年ぶりでしたが、やはりよかったですね。
　当時一番感銘を受けたのは《ユニテ・ダビタシオン・マルセイユ》（1952）でした。物体としてのインパクトももちろんありますが、「世界は幾何学で成り立っている」という歴史的な宣言のように思えて、すごく感動しました。しかし今回の旅行で最も感銘を受けたのは、ベタですが《ロンシャンの教会》（1955）でした。僕が訪れた日は天気が悪く霧がかかっていて、神話のなかの建物のような雰囲気がありました。《ロンシャン》の外観は彫刻的といってもいいような物体感があるのですが、ずっと見ているうちに、物体から空間が生まれてくるのか、空間から物体が生まれてくるのか、ちょうどその境目くらいのきわどい存在であると感じました。原始的というよりも、もっとずっと遡った、ものの始まりそのもののような、そんな不思議な迫力を受けて感動したのです。

藤　森　たしかに《ロンシャンの教会》の平面を高さ4mくらいでぽんと切ると、大きな庇の下の演説台のある空間など、本当は外部なのに内部化して内と外が入り組みよくわからなくなる。藤本さんの作品

もそうで、内と外をはっきりさせないようにしている。特に「安中環境アートフォーラム」(2003)［pp.44, 46］のコンペ案はすごかったですね。プランニングにおいて、空間を閉じないように線が湾曲してずっと続いていく。どうも藤本さんにはそういう傾向があるようですね。

藤　本　最近は平面だけではなく、立体的にもそうなってきています。

藤　森　僕が見たところ、〈虚（の空間）／実（の空間）〉の反転を世界ではじめて試みたのは伊東豊雄さんですね。彼以前にはちょっと思いつかない。藤本さんの「青森県立美術館」設計競技案 (2000)［pp.60, 62］に伊東さんと僕が敏感に反応したのは、作品のなかに〈虚／実〉への意識を感じたからだと思います。伊東さんも〈虚／実〉の反転へのアプローチを始めていましたから、自分と同じ方向性を感じとったのではないでしょうか。藤本さんのそうした〈虚／実〉へ向かう動機はどこからくるのですか？

藤　本　昨年の旅行では、《ロンシャンの教会》に共通していると思った建物が2つありました。ひとつはロンドンで見た《ジョン・ソーンの家》(1808)です。外観は普通なのですが、インテリアがすごい。中に置いてある考古学的、芸術的コレクションがあまりにも多すぎて、空間の中に物が置いてあるのか、物の中に空間がちょっとだけあるのかがわからない。それらが混ざり合って、すごく不思議なんです。

　　　　もうひとつは《ル・トロネ修道院》(1160 – 1190) です。石の塊でつくられているのですが、光のあたり具合なのか、石よりも空間のほうが強く前に出てきて、空間と物の位相が入れ替わるんです。この2つは時代も用途もまったく違う建築なのですが、もしかしたら、普遍的などこかに遡れるのではないかという感触があったのです。

藤森　たしかに優れた建築は、すべてではないけれどもそういった感覚を与えてくれることがありますね。《ル・トロネ修道院》でいうと、その一番大事なことは意外と単純な部分に宿っていると思っています。建物の石の表面には土がごく薄くついてますね。意図的というよりは作業中についてしまったように見える土埃みたいなものは、積んである石全体についていて、これがすごく大事な働きをしている。ここに光が当たると、石という実体の外にその輪郭をなぞったもうひとつの皮膜のような層ができる。《ル・トロネ修道院》の不思議な空間の正体はこれではないかと思っています。

藤本　わかります。そうかもしれませんね。

藤森　僕が〈虚／実〉の反転を伊東さんに強烈に意識したのは、《下諏訪町立諏訪湖博物館・赤彦記念館》(1993)を見た時です。その時、あの建築は彼の《中野本町の家》(1976)をひっくり返したものなのではないかと思ったのです。それを伊東さんに言ったら、まったく気づいてはいなかったが納得してくれた。伊東さんは《せんだいメディアテーク》のことをル・コルビュジエの「ドミノ」だと言うでしょう。たしかにドミノですよ。けれども、あれがドミノのまんまだとすれば、なんのために伊東さんがいるかわからない。最初の案を見てみるとチューブの中が空に抜けていたんですよね。それを見て、これはドミノの柱の内外を反転したものだとすぐにわかりました。柱の中は本当はコンクリートが詰まっているはずですが、イメージのなかで反転して、ああいう世にも珍しい虚実反転伊東ドミノを実現したのだと思います。ああいう反転の仕方があるとは誰も思わなかった。

　もうひとつ、反転問題ですごく興味があるのは、伊東さんに続く建築家たちはなぜ外観を真四角のガラスにするのかということです。彼らはおしなべて「あのガラスはないものとして見て欲しい」と言います。伊東さんの《多摩美術大学新図書館》(2007)もそうで

すが、〈虚／実〉を反転すると、外側が内になっているため、外観のつくりようがなくなってしまう。

藤　本　僕はそこでラッピングをしないなにかをつくりたいと思っています。

藤　森　藤本さんの場合の〈虚／実〉は反転じゃなくて、最初からどちらがどちらなのかわからない。「安中環境アートフォーラム」もそうですし、《T House》(2005)［pp.45, 47］もそうですが、どこが内でどこが外なのかがプラン段階ではわからないのです。

藤　本　《ロンシャンの教会》で穴の開いた壁を外側から見た時に、部屋をつくるように庇が出ている部分があったのですが、特にそこに感動したのです。建物を縦に半分でちょん切ったようで、外部なんだけれども内部的な、ある意味で究極の建築空間のように思えました。これは大分県で建設中の住宅《House N》(2008)［pp.76−81］ですが、毛綱毅曠さんの《反住器》(1972)のように入れ子になっています。ただ、この一番外側は箱なのですが穴だらけで、雨や風が入ってくる。それによってどこまでも無限に外を延長していくという考えです。そうやってどこまでも内と外をずらしていくというか、決定せずにおきたいと考えました。

僕はずっと北海道で育って、大学に入って東京に来たのですが、当時住んでいた街は木造住宅が密集して、路地が曲がりくねって向こうが見えなかったりするので、一歩外に出てもあまり外に出た気がしないような印象のところでした。どうやら僕にはそういう「総体としての住処」に憧れているところはあるようです。

藤　森　《T House》を見た時、この人はこれからどうやって外観をつくっていくんだろうと思ったんです。公共建築は今でも外観が求められる。人は最初に外観で識別しますからね。今のところ《ロンシャンの教会》の大きな庇が理想ということでしょうか？

藤　本　　庇を含めた壁の凹凸の総体ですね。

自然と時間

藤　森　　藤本さんはいくつかの作品で家型を使っていますが、「外観は考えようがありませんが、世間が求めるから世間の言う通り家型にしました」という感じを受けます。あくまで基本的には内部としての外部という方向へ行くのでしょうか？

藤　本　　例えば《"House before House"、東京ガス主催 SUMIKA プロジェクト》（2007－08）［pp.110, 112－113］の場合ですと、建築の外観というよりはむしろ街の外観のようなものが山のように無茶苦茶に立ち上がっています。本来はそういう得体の知れない、人工物とも自然物ともつかないようなものにしたいと思っているのです。例えば、バーナード・ルドフスキーの『建築家なしの建築』（渡辺武信訳、SD 選書、1984）に紹介されている建物が人工物であることは明らかですが、時間が経過していたり、大勢の人が手を加えていたりするので、自然物のような存在になりかけているように見えるんです。そういうものを建築家がつくれないものかと。

藤　森　　それは理想ですが、神様みたいな話になりますよ（笑）。僕は『建築家なしの建築』には載っていなかったすごい建築の写真を見たことがあります。インドネシアにある茅葺屋根の小さな建物なのですが、その柱の一本が本物の木なんです。それを見た時、こりゃかなわんなと思った。これが理想だと思いましたね。要するに、植物と「建築家なしの建築」が一緒になっていたんです。近代以降、われわれは「自分」という毒を飲んで育ってきているわけです。それは「他人」とは違うことに喜びを感じるという毒です。しかし民家の魅力は、集団の無意識を満たしていることにあります。ああいう形が練り上げられ、成立するために、ものすごい

時間をかけているからなんです。その長い時間のなかで、自然化が行なわれるんですね。

美学的なことを言うと、時間を経たものはどこに置いてもしっくり合うんです。骨董品がそうですが、それを現代建築の中に置こうが、本来あった伝統的空間に置こうが、どこに置いても違和感が生じない。その秘密は時間なんです。時間は、個人を超えた、集団的無意識のような感覚に働きかける力がある。それを人為的にできるのかということですよ。

藤本　僕が興味を持っているのは、ある限度を超えた複雑さは、もしかすると集団的無意識に入り込むんじゃないかということです。例えば《情緒障害児短期治療施設》(2006)[pp.28-31, 50-55]はけっこう真面目に設計しているのですが、ふつうに見ればこれだけの数の部屋が無作為にばらまかれてできたように見えるわけです。そうした時に、認識のうえでは新しい人工物に違いないけれども、長い時間をかけて成立したもののように体感されるのではないか。もしかしたらこの感覚が新しい「ものの成り立ち」に関係してくるのではないかと考えています。

モダニズムもある意味では集団の無意識を言い当てたような部分があるわけです。ただそれは、いろいろなものを切り捨てて、ミニマルに整理整頓したものを見せるということだった。それに対して、整理しようとしてもしきれないものを形にすることができるのであれば、それはある種の無意識に働きかける力を持った建築になるのではないかと考えています。

例えば「Primitive Future House」(2001)[pp.23-25]は、床がたくさんあるように見えるけれども、それが床かどうかわからないし、柱なのかもしれない。階段のお化けのようにも見えるし、階段がないようにも見える。そのように、区別される前の状態を形にできる、実体化しえるのではないかと思うんです。そういう希望というか、予感みたいなものに突き動かされている気がします。

藤森　おそらく、その時に大事になってくるのが材料だと思います。例えば肌の色なんてものは遺伝学的には一番どうでもいいことのはずなんですが、それが人間にとって一番大事な識別になっている。実は建築も、重要なのは使われている材料のテクスチャーや色なのではないか。もっと言うと、専門家でない人たちが一番敏感なのはその部分なのです。

例えばミース・ファン・デル・ローエの《レイクショア・ドライブ・アパートメント》（1951）のマリオンを黄色く塗れば、もう阪神タイガースですよ（笑）。あの名作がお笑いにならないのは、それだけのことなんです。黒はペンキの色であって、鉄の色ではないわけですから。近代になってからの議論には、それらに関するものはなかった。そもそも議論する方法がなかったわけです。メタボリズムでも材料の話なんか出てきませんでした。

先ほどの、なぜ骨董品はどんな空間にも合うのかという問題ですが、それは表面の風化という、時間を経たものだけが持っている特権なのです。漆であろうが焼き物であろうが、日が経つと着実に風化していく。われわれの目はそれを識別するんです。だから簡単に言うと、藤本さんは時間の偽造をしたいと言っているのではないでしょうか？

藤本　表面の時間を偽造するのではなくて、「成り立ち」としての時間のようなものを考えているのです。例えば非常に安っぽい材料であったり、明らかに人工的な材料でできていても、その建築を成り立たせているなにかによって、奇妙な、半人工半自然のようなものになる、そういう成り立ちを見つけたいのです。そのときその形式には集団的な無意識につながる時間が宿るのではないかと。

藤森　素材感やテクスチャーのほかに、20世紀の建築理論では一切語られなかったものがあります。それは自然と時間です。目の前にある山や川や空はひとまず置いておいて、建築はこうあるべきだ

と議論してきたわけです。時間についても同じです。

僕は一時、20世紀建築の原理を完成させたのはミースだと考えていましたが、今はヴァルター・グロピウスだと考えています。彼は完全に自然と時間を考えていなかった。批判もしていませんから、要するに捉えていなかったということですね。それが一番の理論的な大問題で、藤本さんもそのことに気づいたんですよ。

そういう意味では、ル・コルビュジエは唯一田舎の人でしたから、海や空を見ていた。けれども彼は絵では語っていますが、言葉では語っていません。なぜかというと、「住宅は住むための機械である」という彼の言葉との連続性が保てないからです。簡単に言うと、機械や飛行機のように建築をつくりましょうと言ってしまったわけですから。そうは言ったけれども、彼の感覚はそこからどんどんずれていく。それをどうしていいかわからない。自然や時間について考えていくと、それこそ〈虚／実〉のような、簡単には解けない問題がたくさん出てくるわけです。

「建築」にはなりたくない

藤 本　僕が今考えているのは、建築というものはすべて「つくられたもの」だけれども、そこを少し超えて、「できてしまったもの」のようにすることはできないかということです。すごく厳密な人工的なプロセスと、「偶然性」「曖昧さ」とが同時に立ち現われるような形式がありえるのではないかと思うのです。

藤 森　僕の経験から言うと、唯一それが可能な状態とは、すべてを自分でつくった時です。《高過庵》（2004）がそうなのですが、とても自由にはつくれないから「できてしまったもの」になるのです。山へ行って支柱に使えそうな木を熱心に探すわけですが、選んだ時点ではこの二股の木に載る平面なんて絶対にわからないわけです。その木を立てて、足場を組んでようやくわかる。自分の意図はつ

ねにあるけれども、現実はその意図通りに動かない。自分の必然や意志や偶然が絡み合いながら形ができてくるわけです。その時に本当の満足ができる。ただ、それをやるのは大変ですよ。僕も結構な数を設計しましたが、すべてを自分でできたのは一作しかないんですから。

藤本　藤森さんは不自由さというものをどのようにお考えでしょうか。自分の技術的な問題、あるいは先がわからずに切り出してきた木の形といった物理的な問題もそうですが、僕には、方法としての不自由さ、またはある種の秩序を成り立たせるものとしての不自由さというか、そういうクリエイティヴな意味での不自由さというものがなにかないかなあという感覚があります。コントロールされえないものがあるがゆえに秩序立っているというような不自由さ。
　全部を自分の思い通りにつくるのではなく、半分は設計するという人工的な作業、半分は建築の形式自身がなりたくてなっていくようななにかがあって、その相互作用のなかで現われる建築に憧れているんです。

藤森　それをやると、先ほど話した集団的無意識というものが必ず出てきます。僕自身も上手くいったりいかなかったりしますね。最近で上手くいったのは《焼杉ハウス》(2007)です。自分で想定していた枠を上手く超えた感じがしたんです。そうしたら、目利きの人たちからは結構ほめられた。素直にいきやすい形、自分に合った形というものがあるのではないかという気はします。けれども、それがなんなのかはわからない。
　藤本さんは「このままやっていると建築っぽくなっちゃうから変えるんです」と言われることがありますが、僕は歴史家だから、歴史上のものと、現代のものは絶対に似ちゃいけないという制約を強く持っているわけです。藤本さんの「建築になりたくない」というのも、そういうことでしょうか？

藤　本　建築になりはじめると嫌なんですよね。途端に小さく小さくなっていくような感覚がどこかにある。建築業界のある論理に回収されてしまうような恐怖というか、そこから自由でいたいという気持ちがある。だからといって、完全に枠組みの外にいたいわけでもなく、その枠組みをちょっと拡張するようなところにいたい。それはそれで大変なんですが、またモチヴェーションにもなっています。

藤　森　建築家の既製の枠に重ならずに進む道はたくさんありますよ。ただ、本当に外れているかどうかは見ればわかります。よく見かけるのは、技術だけ外してるな、とかね。しかし、技術だけ外してあとはみんな同じというのでは少し寂しい。もちろんそれだけでも大変なんですが、そうでない枠の外し方をしてもらいたいですね。その点、藤本さんの志はいいと思います。いま世界でそういうことに挑戦している人はいるのでしょうか？

藤　本　僕はフランク・O・ゲーリーの《MITレイ＆マリア・スタータ・センター》（2004）を見た時に、これは今までの建築という人工物の概念をちょっとだけ拡張しているのではないかと思いました。あれも徹底的にデザインしたものですが、実際に体験すると、ジャングルのなかにいるような生き生きとした感じがするんですよね。すごく新鮮な体験でした。そのような、人工物と自然物の間を成立させたいと思っているのですが、この意識はもしかしたら非常に日本的なものなのかもしれません。以前、銀閣寺の庭を見た時には、そういうことをすごく感じましたね。人間が手を加えた自然がすごくパワーを持っていて衝撃的だったのです。僕にとっての理想の建築とは、もしかしたらそういう庭のようなものなのかもしれません。屋根もないような。

原風景と建築

藤　森　庭や管理された緑は大きな働きをします。しかしなかなか難しい。

自然物は人工物よりも強く、あらゆる建築を植木鉢と化してしまうからです。世界に上手くいった例があるとすれば、芝棟だけではないかと僕は思います。花が咲いた時、建築と植物がバランスを取った時の美しさは本当にすばらしい。人工物と自然物が一体化しながらお互いを引き立て合う、夢のような状況です。一般に庭はわれわれよりずっと歴史が長いし、われわれのことをまったく考えていない、無遠慮なものですよね。

藤　本　銀閣寺もそうですが、庭はふつう植物で成り立っていますよね。しかし先ほどもお話したように、工業製品である建築材料のみを使ってその「成り立ち」だけを実現する、庭のような建築を生み出せないかと考えています。それもまた夢のような話なのですが。

藤　森　竜安寺の石庭のように、周囲に植物があれば大丈夫でしょう。あれが都会の真ん中にあったら馬鹿みたいですが、周囲が緑と山だから成立しているわけです。もしくは、水を使えばやりようがあると思います。

藤　本　もうひとつ好きな庭に関する造形に、イサム・ノグチの「プレイグラウンド」シリーズがあります。あれも人工物と自然物の関係へのアプローチだったのだろうと考えています。

藤　森　シリーズで実現した最大のものは北海道の《モエレ沼公園》（2005）ですが、間違いなくそうだと思いますね。彼は20世紀のアメリカが生んだ最高の彫刻家でしょう。僕は彼の作品をかなり見ていますが、最高傑作は自作の彼自身の墓だと思っています。香川県庵治のアトリエ前庭に丘をつくり、その頂上に遺骨が入った大きな石が置いてある。これを見た時に、彼は「物が存在する」という状態を突き詰めて表現したかったのではないかと感じました。選ばれた自然のなかに人工的な物が存在することの究

極の状態に行き着いたのだと思います。

藤本さんは「夢のような話」と言いますが、なにか目処はあるわけですか？

藤　本　　イメージはあるんです。武満徹が尺八の師匠に「尺八の音で一番理想的な音はどういう音か」と訊いたら、師匠は「風が竹林を吹き流れる音だ」と答えたそうです。尺八はいわゆる人工物であり人間が吹くものですが、師匠はそういう瞬間をつくることができるに違いないと考えているわけで、すごくいいなあと思います。ですから、人間が自然に化け、自然が人間に化けるイメージと言ったらよいのでしょうか。

藤　森　　やはり藤本さんはなかなか面白いことを考えていますね。僕は、人のなかにはなにか造形に繋がる原型のようなものがあるのではないかと思っています。それはおそらく子どもの時に見たもののなかにあります。子ども時代にいろんなものを見て、自分の好き／嫌いがだんだんとわかってくるわけですが、若い時は向上心もあって自分にはないものに憧れるものです。そしてある歳になると、もっと深いところにある好みのようなものがだんだん出てくる。それが子どもの頃から蓄積してきたものと上手く繋がるのが一番いいんですね。

人はそうしたイメージを使っている時はなんの不安も感じず、どうやってこれを使おうかという面白さだけを感じます。ですから、藤本さんのなかにも無意識的なイメージがあるわけです。しかしそれは、ほかの人と同じものを見てきた経験のなかで君のなかにかたちづくられたものですから、間違いなく集団的無意識に通じている。それが今後も自分とどこかで繋がり続け、建築として出していくことができれば上手くいきますよ。

Artificial Architecture, Natural Architecture: Dialogue Summary

Terunobu Fujimori [Architectural historian, Architect] × Sou Fujimoto

Translated by Kaz Yoneda

As a student, Sou Fujimoto was interested in Le Corbusier. While he was awestruck by "Unité d'Habitation in Marseilles" (1952) in his youth, during his recent trip to France the admiration shifted to "Chapelle Notre-Dame-du-Haut de Ronchamp" (1955). Fujimoto was transfixed by the sculptural solidity of Ronchamp, and the way it evoked a sense of an enigmatic presence between space created by mass, or mass borne from space, and was moved by this strange compulsion as if witnessing the genesis of matter itself.

Terunobu Fujimori points out the similarities between Ronchamp and Fujimoto's work. When looking at the plan of Ronchamp at a height of 4 meters, clear delineation of the interior and exterior is obscured by convolutions of vertical surfaces. Fujimoto's work shares this tendency, especially in the winning proposal for "Annaka Art Forum Competition" (2003) ［pp.44, 46］ and "T House" (2005) ［pp.45, 47］. Energetic intonation of external wall disengages the confinement of interiority by extending the corporeal and sensorial boundaries. Fujimoto's proclivity lies not in the legitimization of sinuous forms, but in the negation of rigid inside/outside hierarchy.

Fujimori states that the first architect in Japan to address the idea of architectural inversion was Toyo Ito. He also analyzes that the reason Ito responds positively to Fujimoto's architecture is because he recognizes similar underlying motives toward architecture. Fujimori adds that Ito's "Shimosuwa Suwako Museum Akahiko Memorial Hall" (1993) is an inversion of his earlier work, "House in Nakano-Honmachi" (1976). Likewise, the latticed columnar tubes of "Sendai

Mediatheque" (2000) create an inverse condition of Le Corbusier's "Maison Domino."

Naturally, when space is inverted, the interior becomes the exterior. For this reason, Ito and like-minded architects envelop their architecture in glass, an immaterial medium, to imply a continuous landscape. In contrast, Fujimoto proposes the creation of architecture that does not require a "wrapping." Fujimori distinguishes Ito's architecture as a consequence of systematic inversion, while Fujimoto's architecture blurs interiority and exteriority from the onset. Fujimoto's recent attempts to envision such infinite outward expansion can be seen in works such as "House N" (2008) [pp.76-81].

Fujimoto, who came from a gridded city in Hokkaido, moved to Tokyo when he began his college education. Living in Tokyo where wooden houses and narrow alleys intermingled, he discovered a sense of "dwelling as a totality", and considered this protean state of non-separation between architecture and the city, the artificial and the natural phenomena, to be one of his ideals. This perspective towards urbanism and city influences his architecture. "House before House", SUMIKA project by Tokyo Gas (2007-08) [pp.110, 112-113] is less an exterior of "architecture," characterized by "city"-like exterior emerging like a mountainous landscape.

Fujimoto questions if contemporaries can generate architecture, which is indubitably an artificial construct, capable of transforming itself to resemble a natural construct as temporal effects accumulate and by the involvement of numerous hands, such as those introduced in Bernard Rudofsky's *Architecture without Architects* (1964). Fujimori responds that the strength of "architecture without architects" is that it fills the subconscious necessities of the masses, and therefore the natural transformation of built form is accomplished over myriads of time. On the other hand, Fujimori allegorizes that by consuming a poison of self-importance and thus deriving pleasure in identifying "oneself" different than "others," contemporaries have diminished their ability to form this sense of subliminal collectivity. To this, Fujimoto hypothesizes that certain sophisticated complexities are still recognized by the collective subconsciousness. Taking his "Children's Center for Psychiatric Rehabilitation" (2006) [pp.28-31, 50-55] as an example, the precisely configured plan also gives an impression that the individual cubes were placed spontaneously. It also consists of clearly man-made materials. However, Fujimoto believes that people can feel a certain sense of "the becoming of things" that came into existence over a long period of time.

Fujimori problematizes the methodology used to obtain this highly developed condition of naturalness. He suggests, "People respond most sensitively to the surface of things. In order to vigorously simulate the passing of time, to actualize 'the forming of objects,' selection of materials, color, and texture is a key." To this, Fujimoto counters, "I am less interested in the mimicry of temporal affects on surfaces, and more in formulating *arrière-pensée* towards temporality."

Furthermore, Fujimori contends that materiality and texture as well as nature and temporality were rarely discussed in twentieth century architectural theory. Consequently, it was fitting that Walter Gropius epitomized the architectural basis of the twentieth century, as he was indifferent to issues of nature and time. Fujimoto's idea of competing with time and its simulation originates from his realization of those fundamental flaws in Modernist ideology.

Likewise, Fujimoto disdains his works becoming "architecture." That is to say, he senses his ideas are congealed as they are reduced to unrelated theories within the profession, becoming platitudinous "architecture." He wants to see "architecture" liberated. In Frank O. Gehry's "Stata Center, MIT" (2004), Fujimoto sensed that it expanded the potential of "architecture" as artifice. Categorical artificiality of its design generated spaces with the vivacity of wandering through a jungle. The sense of "nature altered by human hand" is epitomized by Japanese gardens. With this, Fujimoto projects his ideal architecture to be roofless and garden-like. To Fujimori's inquiry about generating such an embryonic architecture, Fujimoto responded by recounting a vignette; "Toru Takemitsu once asked his master of the shakuhachi, a vertical bamboo flute, 'What would be the most ideal sound produced by this instrument?' His master responded that it was the sound of the wind breezing through a bamboo grove. The shakuhachi is an artificial object blown by a human being, but the master believed that it was possible to recreate an analogical moment. I find that to be extraordinary, as if to imagine a human being metamorphosing into nature and nature metamorphosing into a human being."

Lastly, Fujimori says, "I believe that there is a primordial form from which things are derived." He adds that this form is from something we have all witnessed in our childhood. Forms derived from memory are connected to the collective subconsciousness as it is constantly informed by numerous and shared experiences within a society. Fujimori asserts that Fujimoto will thrive as long as he is able to manifest this ubiquitous and causal awareness in his architecture.

Data

Date	Title	Location	Program	Structure	Pages
2007-10	武蔵野美術大学美術資料図書館新棟および旧棟建築工事	東京、日本	図書館、美術館	鉄骨	93-97
2006-09	Tokyo Apartment	東京、日本	集合住宅	木造	111, 114-115
2007-08	"House before House"、東京ガス主催 SUMIKA プロジェクト	栃木、日本	住宅	鉄骨	110, 112-113
2008	House N	大分、日本	住宅	RC	76-81
2005-08	熊本アートポリス次世代木造バンガロー	熊本、日本	住宅	木造	121
2008-	House/Garden	栃木、日本	住宅	RC	102-103
2008-	Empty House	栃木、日本	住宅	鉄骨	87
2008	Between House and Tree、プロジェクト	北海道、日本	パヴィリオン	鉄骨	116-117
2007	House O	千葉、日本	住宅	RC	34-35, 38-41
2007	House Inside-Out Tree	神奈川、日本	住宅	RC	64-65, 68
2007	House NA	東京、日本	住宅	鉄骨	69
2007-	House H	東京、日本	住宅	RC	72-73
2007-	House OM	神奈川、日本	住宅	鉄骨	98
2007	Spiral House、プロジェクト	東京、日本	住宅	RC	99
2007	House I、プロジェクト	東京、日本	住宅	RC	104-105
2006	情緒障害児短期治療施設	北海道、日本	医療施設	RC	28-31, 50-55
2006	Diagonal Walls/登別のグループホーム	北海道、日本	医療施設	木造	42-43
2006	7/2 House	北海道、日本	住宅	木造	58-59
2006-	聖台病院増築、プロジェクト	北海道、日本	医療施設	RC	32-33
2006	House/Forest、プロジェクト	東京、日本	住宅	RC	106-107
2005	T House	群馬、日本	住宅	木造	45, 47
2005-	北海道のアトリエ	北海道、日本	住宅	木造	70-71
2003	伊達の援護寮	北海道、日本	医療施設	鉄骨	56-57
2003	安中環境アートフォーラム、プロジェクト、コンペ最優秀賞	群馬、日本	多目的施設	鉄骨	44, 46
2002	Glass Cloud、プロジェクト	N/A	住宅	鉄骨	84-85
2001	Primitive Future House、プロジェクト	N/A	住宅	鉄骨	23-25
2000	青森県立美術館、コンペ優秀賞	青森、日本	美術館	RC	60, 62
2000	M 病院デイケアセンター、プロジェクト	北海道、日本	医療施設	RC	86
1999	聖台病院新病棟	北海道、日本	医療施設	RC	61, 63
1995	House of Infinity、新建築住宅コンペ案	N/A	住宅	N/A	88-89

Date	Title	Location	Program	Structure	Pages
2007-10	New Library and Museum of Musashino Art University	Tokyo, Japan	Library, Art Museum	Steel	93-97
2006-09	Tokyo Apartment	Tokyo, Japan	Multifamily Housing	Wood	111, 114-115
2007-08	"House before House", SUMIKA project by Tokyo Gas	Tochigi, Japan	Residential	Steel	110, 112-113
2008	House N	Oita, Japan	Residential	RC	76-81
2005-08	Next Generation Wooden Bungalows	Kumamoto, Japan	Residential	Wood	121
2008-	House/Garden	Tochigi, Japan	Residential	RC	102-103
2008-	Empty House	Tochigi, Japan	Residential	Steel	87
2008	Between House and Tree, project	Hokkaido, Japan	Pavilion	Steel	116-117
2007	House O	Chiba, Japan	Residential	RC	34-35, 38-41
2007	House Inside-Out Tree	kanagawa, Japan	Residential	RC	64-65, 68
2007	House NA	Tokyo, Japan	Residential	Steel	69
2007-	House H	Tokyo, Japan	Residential	RC	72-73
2007-	House OM	kanagawa, Japan	Residential	Steel	98
2007	Spiral House, project	Tokyo, Japan	Residential	RC	99
2007	House I, project	Tokyo, Japan	Residential	RC	104-105
2006	Children's Center for Psychiatric Rehabilitation	Hokkaido, Japan	Healthcare	RC	28-31, 50-55
2006	Diagonal Walls/Group Home in Noboribetsu	Hokkaido, Japan	Healthcare	Wood	42-43
2006	7/2 House	Hokkaido, Japan	Residential	Wood	58-59
2006-	Seidai Hospital New Wing, project	Hokkaido, Japan	Healthcare	RC	32-33
2006	House/Forest, project	Tokyo, Japan	Residential	RC	106-107
2005	T House	Gunma, Japan	Residential	Wood	45, 47
2005-	Atelier/House in Hokkaido	Hokkaido, Japan	Residential	Wood	70-71
2003	Rehabilitation Dormitory in Hokkaido	Hokkaido, Japan	Healthcare	Steel	56-57
2003	Annaka Art Forum, project, Competition 1st Prize	Gunma, Japan	Multipurpose	Steel	44, 46
2002	Glass Cloud, project	N/A	Residential	Steel	84-85
2001	Primitive Future House, project	N/A	Residential	Steel	23-25
2000	Aomori Prefectural Art Museum, Competition 2nd Prize	Aomori, Japan	Museum	RC	60, 62
2000	M-Hospital Day Care Center, project	Hokkaido, Japan	Healthcare	RC	86
1999	Seidai Hospital Annex	Hokkaido, Japan	Healthcare	RC	61, 63
1995	House of Infinity, Shinkenchiku Competition	N/A	Residentia	N/A	88-89

Profile

藤本壮介

藤本壮介建築設計事務所
web site：http://www.sou-fujimoto.com/

1971　北海道生まれ
1994　東京大学工学部建築学科 卒業
2000　藤本壮介建築設計事務所設立
2008　京都大学、東京理科大学、昭和女子大学非常勤講師

受　賞

2008　JIA 日本建築大賞（情緒障害児短期治療施設）
2007　Architectural Record "Design Vanguard"
2007　AR AWARDS 2007 優秀賞（House O）
2007　2007 KENNETH F. BROWN ARCHITECTURE DESIGN AWARD 入選
2006　AR AWARDS 2006 大賞（情緒障害児短期治療施設）
2006　AR AWARDS 2006 優秀賞（7/2 House）
2006　平成 18 年東京建築士会住宅建築賞金賞（T House）
2005　くまもとアートポリス設計競技 2005：次世代モクバン最優秀賞
2005　AR AWARDS 2005 優秀賞（伊達援護寮）
2005　AR AWARDS 2005 佳作（T House）
2004　JIA 新人賞 2004（伊達援護寮）
2003　安中環境アートフォーラム国際設計競技最優秀賞
2000　青森県立美術館設計競技優秀賞

Photo Credit
阿野太一　　38, 39, 42, 43, 47, 50-51, 53, 54-55, 56-57
谷本　夏　　112-113, 114-115
エドモンド・サムナー　　34-35
新建築写真部　　58-59

Profile

Sou Fujimoto

Sou Fujimoto Architects
Web site: http://www.sou-fujimoto.com/

1971	Born in Hokkaido, Japan
1994	Graduated from The University of Tokyo, Faculty of Engineering, Department of Architecture
2000	Established Sou Fujimoto Architects in Tokyo
2008	Lecturer Critic at Kyoto University, Tokyo University of Science, Showa Women's University

Awards

2008	Japanese Institute of Architects Grand Prize 2007 (Children's Center for Psychiatric Rehabilitation)
2007	Architectural Record "Design Vanguard"
2007	AR Awards 2007 "Highly Commended" (House O)
2007	2007 KENNETH F. BROWN ARCHITECTURE DESIGN AWARD Honorable Mention (Children's Center for Psychiatric Rehabilitation)
2006	AR Awards 2006 "Grand Prize" (Children's Center for Psychiatric Rehabilitation)
2006	AR Awards 2006 "Highly Commended" (7/2 House)
2006	Tokyo Society of Architects and Building Engineers, Residential Architecture 2006 Gold Award (T House)
2005	"1st Prize" in Next Generation Wooden Bungalow Competition in Kumamoto
2005	AR Awards 2005 "Highly Commended" (Rehabilitation Dormitory in Hokkaido)
2005	AR Awards 2005 "Honorable Mention" (T House)
2004	Japanese Institute of Architects New Face Award 2004
2003	"1st Prize" in International Design Competition for Annaka Art Forum
2000	"2nd Prize" in Design Competition for the Aomori Prefectural Art Museum

Photo Credit

Daichi Ano   38, 39, 42, 43, 47, 50-51, 53, 54-55, 56-57
Natsu Tanimoto   112-113, 114-115
Edmond Sumner   34-35
Shinkenchiku-sha   58-59

現代建築家コンセプト・シリーズ1
藤本壮介 原初的な未来の建築

| 発 行 日 | 2008年4月15日 初版第1刷発行 |
| | 2009年3月20日 第2版第4刷発行 |

著　者　藤本壮介、伊東豊雄、五十嵐太郎、藤森照信

発 行 者　秋山泉

発 行 所　INAX出版
　　　　　〒104-0031 東京都中央区京橋3-6-18
　　　　　TEL.03-5250-6571　FAX.03-5250-6549

企画・編集　メディア・デザイン研究所

造　　本　町口覚

デ ザ イ ン　伊野耕一（match and company, inc.）

印刷・製本　凸版印刷株式会社

ISBN978-4-87275-148-2 C0352
©2008 by Sou Fujimoto, Printed in Japan

乱丁・落丁本はINAX出版までお送りください。
送料負担にてお取り替えいたします。